A Cooks Tour of
Rabbit Ridge Winery
and Vineyards

CENTRAL COAST PRESS

San Luis Obispo, California

ISBN 1-930401-17-5

Printed in China

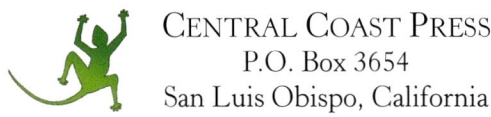

CENTRAL COAST PRESS
P.O. Box 3654
San Luis Obispo, California

CONTENTS

FOREWORD

I began writing this cookbook years ago when I was single. I was so passionate about food that I would plan my day around every meal. For me, eating divine food was the most important luxury I could have. I was fortunate to have had a career that exposed me to great dining and cuisine in Manhattan, New York. It was this experience that fueled my career as a caterer in my late 20's. Through the years I have explored many different styles of food preparation. However, the one thing that has stayed consistent in my development as a cook, is my expectation for perfection in the kitchen. It is this desire for perfection that has caused this book to take 15 years to write. I am now 42, married to Erich Russell, founder and winemaker of Rabbit Ridge, and I am blessed with the most adorable daughter who is my angel and my guiding light. Although I no longer have the time to cook as elaborately as I did before I ran a winery with my husband, great food and wine are still my passion. This book is filled with simple and not so simple recipes. Use them for those special occasions, and for the every day meal. I have paired many of the recipes with our wines as a suggestion, but as always, drink what you enjoy.

There are a few ingredients that I feel very strongly about. Substituting these staples will dramatically change the recipe. Therefore, please consider the following. First, high quality extra virgin olive oil is a must. It can be pricey, but regular olive oil does not have the best flavor. Second, buy high quality cheese, like Reggiano Parmigano, Grana Padano, and fresh mozzarella. Again, these fine cheeses make all the difference. Third, season the recipe correctly. Use fresh herbs, if possible, and try not to over or under salt. Finally, and obviously, use a very good wine to cook with. In some instances, the wine I have suggested as a pairing should be the wine used in the recipe.

Cheers and Salute'.

Young vines planted one week earlier in the Live Oak Vineyard, Paso Robles, California.

PLANTING SEASON AND APPETIZERS

Erich's Antipasti	8
Caviar, stacked and served with Assorted Accompaniments	10
Crostini with Liver Pâté	12
Crostini with Artichokes	12
Crostini with Mushrooms	12
Crostini with Olive Tapenade	12
Bruschetta	14
Blue Cheese Mousse drizzled with Honey	15
Crabmeat on Belgian Endive	17
Hummus	18
Mushrooms, marinated in Extra Virgin Olive Oil and Balsamic Vinegar and Herbs	21
Olives, marinated in Italian Vinaigrette	24
Olive Tapenade	25

Erich's Antipasti

The Italian Appetizer – "Antipasti" – meaning: Before Pasta- is a wonderful way to enjoy a variety of vegetables, seafood, cured meats and cheese. While visiting the Piedmont region of Italy in May 1999, Erich and I found that most antipasti were an assortment of pickled fresh fish. I prefer vegetables, olives, a few meats and cheese.

<u>Step One</u>   <u>Serves 8-12</u>

1 cup marinated olives -	**Page 24**
1 cup marinated mushrooms -	**Page 21**
2 grilled red peppers -	**Page 41**
2 grilled yellow peppers -	**Page 41**
½ lb. salami, sliced thin	
Braised artichoke hearts -	**Page 34**
¼ lb. Parma prosciutto, sliced thin	
1 cup pepperocini peppers, drained	
¼ lb. Parmigiano-Reggiano cheese, cut	
in chunks	
Assorted bread sticks and loafs	

Drain olives and mushrooms. Place in decorative bowls on a large platter. Decorate the olives and mushrooms with the other ingredients. Serve with toothpicks.

Recommended Wine

Rabbit Ridge Dolcetto, Barbera, Sangiovese

Caviar with Assorted Accompaniments

We love fine caviar served with the traditional chopped egg, and crème fraîche. While visiting San Francisco, I enjoyed this famous hors d' oeuvre, stacked, using diced potatoes as a base. It is not only beautiful to look at, but extremely delicious. Only use high quality caviar for this dish. Frozen hash browns can be used to speed up this recipe. However, I do not think they taste as good as freshly diced potatoes.

__Step One__ - Make Crème Fraîche- one day ahead or purchase ready-made.

__Serves 2__

1 cup heavy whipping cream

1 cup sour cream

1 pinch sugar

See page 59 for method. Place chilled crème fraîche in a large pastry bag fitted with a plain medium-sized open tip. Place bag in refrigerator.

__Step Two__

2 large baking potatoes

3 tablespoons unsalted butter

2 tablespoon extra virgin olive oil

Salt and pepper to taste

Peel and finely dice potato. In a large non-stick sauté pan, warm butter and olive oil until shimmering. Place potatoes in the pan and season with salt and pepper. Lightly brown diced potatoes on all sides. With a slotted spoon, remove potatoes and place on a paper bag to drain. Set aside to cool. Wrap in plastic wrap. Do not refrigerate.

__Step Three__

2 eggs, hard boiled, cooled

4 tablespoons fresh chives, cut very small with scissors

3 ounces Beluga, Osetra, or other fine caviar.

Place the hard-boiled eggs in a mini processor and finely chop. Put the chopped eggs in a bowl and stir in chives. Set aside. Have the caviar ready for assembly as shown on the following page.

Recommended Wine
Rabbit Ridge Blanc de noir, Sparkling Wine, Champagne, Premium Vodka

Caviar mold assembly

If you do not have a stacking mold, cover the bottom and ½ of the sides of a Rabbit Ridge wine bottle with plastic wrap. Tear off one large piece of aluminum foil. Fold the foil into fourths. Foil should be about 2-3 inches tall. Wrap the aluminum foil around the Rabbit Ridge wine bottle. Do not wrap the foil too tightly. Loosely seal the foil with tape. Slide the foil mold off the bottle. Place 1 foil mold on each plate and fill the bottom of each mold with ½ of the potato mixture. Pipe a small circle of crème fraîche on top of the potatoes. Spoon ½ of the egg mixture on top of the potatoes.

Press down on the eggs with the bottom of the wine bottle that had been covered in plastic wrap. Pipe enough crème fraîche on top of eggs to cover entire surface. Carefully, smooth the crème flat. Layer the other ½ of the potatoes on top of the crème. Follow with the other ½ of the egg mixture. Press down again with the bottle. Add more crème fraîche, completely covering the egg mixture. Top the crème with 1 to 1½ oz. caviar on each mold. Carefully smooth the top of the caviar with a plastic spatula. Gently remove tape and unwrap. Serve with a caviar spoon, or any non-metal spoon. Serve immediately.

Crostini with Liver Pâté

Crostini, which means, "toast," are appetizers made from toasted bread topped with a savory topping. This is a very simple and delicious liver paté. My mother added allspice and thyme, which I think, gives this paté even more "zip." This is a perfect topping for crostini.

Step One

Makes about 2.5 cups

2 cloves garlic, minced
1 large shallot, minced
2 tablespoons unsalted butter
2 teaspoons tomato paste

Step Two
16 oz. cooked liver paté, or liver mousse
8 tablespoons unsalted butter, soft
½ cup veal or beef stock
¼ cup brandy
1/8 cup finely minced green onions
** (scallions)**
1 teaspoon capers, rinsed and drained
¼ teaspoon allspice
2 teaspoons fresh thyme leaves
Salt and pepper to taste

Grilled bread rounds, toasted

Saute garlic and shallots in butter until soft, about 2 minutes. Add tomato paste and cook 1 more minute. Set aside for step two.

Place all ingredients in a food processor. Process until smooth. Serve on grilled or toasted bread rounds for crostini, in a ramekin, on toast points, crackers or apples. Chill well before serving.

Crostini with Artichokes
Place braised artichokes (page 34), on toasted or grilled bread rounds. Drizzle with high quality olive oil. Serves 4

Crostini with Mushrooms
Place sautéed mushrooms (page 47), on toasted or grilled bread rounds. Drizzle with high quality olive oil. Serves 4

Crostini with Olive Tapenade
Place Olive Tapenade (page 25), on toasted or grilled bread rounds. Drizzle with high quality olive oil. Serves 4

Recommended Wine
Rabbit Ridge Sangiovese, Syrah

Vineyard crews pound in the grape stakes which will serve as the support for future vines. (Right)

Completed staking is ready for installation of irrigation lines. (Below)

Bruschetta with Tomato

Bruschetta are appetizers made from grilled bread, rubbed with garlic, and drizzled with olive oil. We love bruschetta made with fresh tomatoes and basil from our garden in California.

Step One

3 large tomatoes

Step Two

¼ cup fresh basil, chopped
1 teaspoon extra virgin olive oil
½ teaspoon balsamic vinegar
Salt and pepper to taste

Step Three

1-2 baguettes or bread of choice
6-8 whole garlic cloves, cut in half
Extra virgin olive oil

Serves 8

Seed and dice the tomatoes. Place in a plastic container.

Combine remaining ingredients. Add to tomatoes and toss. Place in refrigerator for 30 minutes. Drain if necessary.

Slice bread ¼ inch thick. Grill or toast bread until marked. Rub top side of toast with raw garlic. Top with tomato mixture, drizzle with olive oil and serve immediately.

Recommended Wine
Rabbit Ridge Sauvignon Blanc, Red Zinfandel

Blue Cheese Mousse drizzled with Honey

I tasted something like this at a wedding reception years ago. The combination of high quality blue cheese and cream cheese are absolutely divine.

Step One

Serves 8

8 ounces cream cheese, softened

4 ounces crumbled Blue Cheese

1 tablespoon heavy cream

Juice of ½ lemon

1 teaspoon Worcestershire sauce

2 tablespoons Rabbit Ridge Chardonnay or vermouth

½ teaspoon garlic powder

1 dash of white pepper

1 dash of cayenne pepper

1 dash of salt

Combine all ingredients in a food processor and blend. Add more cream if necessary. Line a small ramekin or small serving dish with plastic wrap. Spoon mixture into ramekin and seal. Press firmly to shape. Chill one hour.

Step Two

½ cup chopped pecans

Honey to taste

1-2 tablespoons Honey Crackers or vegetables crudités

Unmold cheese mixture onto a serving plate. Remove wrap. Sprinkle with chopped pecans. Drizzle honey on top. Serve cold with crackers or vegetables.

Recommended Wine

Rabbit Ridge Red Zinfandel, Cabernet Sauvignon

Trenches are dug for irrigation lines prior to planting new vines. End posts are put in place and irrigation pipes are ready to bury prior to stringing irrigation and fruiting wire.

Crabmeat on Belgian Endive

Lump crabmeat is always wonderful. In this recipe, I have combined it with my herb/garlic cream cheese, stuffed it into endive leaves and topped it with a colorful garnish. Freeze extra cheese mixture for another use.

<u>Step One</u> - Make garlic cream cheese   *<u>Serves 4</u>*

2 tablespoons butter

4 cloves garlic, minced

2 shallots, minced

8 ounces cream cheese, softened

3 ounces plain goat cheese, softened

1 teaspoon garlic powder

½ teaspoon Lawry's seasoning salt

1 teaspoon fresh parsley, minced

1 teaspoon fresh dill, minced

1 teaspoon fresh basil, minced

½ teaspoon fresh thyme, minced

Sauté garlic and shallots in butter. Place garlic, shallots, cream cheese, goat cheese, garlic powder and seasoning salt in a processor. Mix thoroughly. Place mixture in a bowl and add herbs. Stir to combine.

<u>Step Two</u>

1 cup fresh lump crabmeat

¼ cup garlic/herb cream cheese (step 1)

2 tablespoons mayonnaise

Combine mayonnaise and cream cheese mixture. Gently fold in crabmeat.

<u>Step Three</u>

Toast points or crackers

1 large red pepper, diced small

Alfalfa sprouts for garnish

Scoop crabmeat onto toast points or crackers. Place red pepper and sprouts on top. Chill 30 minutes. Serve cold.

<u>Recommended Wine</u>
Rabbit Ridge Sauvignon blanc, Chardonnay

Hummus

This is a healthy and tasty dip. Make sure to carefully add a tiny bit of reserved liquid back into the pureed mixture so that it does not become runny.

Step One

2 cups chick peas, in liquid

Step Two

1 - 2 large garlic cloves, minced
¼ cup chicken stock
3 tablespoons Tahini (can be found in
   oriental section of grocery store)
Juice of 1-2 lemons
Tabasco to taste
Salt and pepper to taste

Step Three

Belgian endive leaves, washed, dried
   and separated or grilled pita bread,
   cut into triangles
Pinch of paprika

Serves 8

Drain chickpeas and reserve liquid. Place drained chickpeas and 1 tablespoon of reserved liquid in a processor and puree until smooth.

Add remaining ingredients to chickpeas and pulse to combine. Add only as much lemon juice as needed. Add only as much reserved liquid needed to achieve a smooth consistency. Chill.

Spoon hummus into endive leaves. Or, serve hummus in a bowl surrounded with grilled pita. Sprinkle with paprika. Serve cold.

Variation 1- Add 1 tablespoon fresh minced basil to step two. Process to combine.

Variation 2- Add 2 tablespoons chopped black, pitted Kalamata (or other dark olive) to step two. Process to combine. Serve on a small plate. Drizzle with high quality olive oil. Serve with bread sticks or crackers.

Recommended Wine
Rabbit Ridge Sauvignon blanc

Crews begin the long process of cutting drip hose.

A drip hose gadget aids the crew in measuring even sized pieces.

Yards of drip line are cut into exact 45 inch pieces. This length ensures deep penetration to the vine's root.

When we purchased the Vista Serrano vineyard, part of the land contained an old fashioned trellis system that we converted to a modern "Lyre" system. (Above)

Winemaker Erich shows the best place to install drip hose for new vines. (Below)

Mushrooms, marinated with Extra Virgin Olive Oil, Balsamic Vinegar and Herbs

These mushrooms look great served in a large crystal bowl with toothpicks.

Step One

¼ cup white wine vinegar

¼ cup sherry

1/8 cup balsamic vinegar

1 cup extra virgin olive oil

½ cup with capers with 1 tablespoon brine

6 cloves garlic, minced

1 teaspoon dried fennel, ground fine

½ cup fresh basil, chopped

Salt and pepper to taste

½ cup fresh parsley, chopped

¼ cup Rabbit Ridge Merlot or other
   red wine

Serves 8

Combine all ingredients in a large zip-lock baggie or plastic container.

Step Two

1 - 2 lbs. fresh mushrooms

1 tablespoon extra virgin olive oil

Clean mushrooms and cut off stems. If using small mushrooms, leave whole. If larger, cut into bite size pieces. Toss mushrooms with olive oil. Place on a sheet pan with sides and broil 5 minutes. Drain off all liquid. Place in the zip-lock baggie or plastic container from step one and marinate overnight, turning occasionally. Drain and serve.

Recommended Wine
Rabbit Ridge Merlot or other Red Wine

Occasionally some vines don't survive. In the spring, they will be replaced with these new vines.

New vines cascade down the steep Live Oak terrain. (below)

Olives, marinated in Herb Vinaigrette

I created this marinated olive recipe after my trip to Cannes, France with Erich. We enjoyed these tiny olives served with champagne on the beach in southern France.

<u>**Step One**</u> - **Marinade**

½ **cup Vinaigrette, page 150**
4 large cloves garlic, pressed and minced
1-2 tablespoons fresh cilantro, chopped
1 teaspoon each- dried fennel, basil, oregano
1 tablespoon lemon zest, minced

<u>**Step Two**</u>

2 cups Nicoise French olives (or any other unbrined black olives), rinsed and drained

<u>Serves 4</u>

Combine ingredients in a plastic bowl or large baggie.

Place olives in marinade. Marinate overnight. Drain and serve.

Recommended Wine
Rabbit Ridge Sauvignon blanc, Blance de noir, Sparkling Wine or Champagne

Olive Tapenade

This is another item that is used for crostini in Italy. After pureeing, spread a thin layer on bread rounds, or simply serve with crackers. Serve cold.

Step One

Serves 4

½ cup prepared vinaigrette - page 150
1 teaspoon fresh basil, minced
½ teaspoon fresh oregano, minced
1 can pitted ripe olives, drained (16 oz.)
½ cup pitted black Greek or Italian
   olives, drained

Stir herbs into vinaigrette. Place olives in marinade and refrigerate overnight. Drain.

Step Two

1 teaspoon prepared yellow mustard
1 tablespoon capers, drained
1 teaspoon anchovy paste
1 teaspoon mustard seeds
Salt and pepper to taste
A drizzle of extra virgin olive oil

Place olives, prepared mustard, capers, mustard seeds and anchovy paste in processor. Process until smooth. Add some marinade if needed. Add salt, pepper and olive oil and chill.

Step Three

Assorted bread or crackers

Slice bread. Spread olive tapenade on bread for crostini or serve as a dip with crackers.

Recommended Wine
Rabbit Ridge Allure, Sangiovese

Vines are taken from flats and carefully placed in the ground.

A perfectly planted new vine. (Left)

The Texas Road Vineyard ready to string irrigation lines. (Below)

GROWING SEASON and VEGETABLES

The 1 meter by 2 meter plantings look like hedges.

By early spring, young vines are racing up the vineyard wire to attain maximum sun exposure.

Asparagus Laced with Balsamic Vinegar

Make sure you buy asparagus that have firm stems and tightly closed tips.

<u>**Step One**</u>   <u>*Serves 4*</u>

¼ cup balsamic vinegar
1 teaspoon extra virgin olive oil

Place balsamic vinegar in a small sauce-pan. Bring to a low simmer and reduce to 1/8 cup. Remove from heat. Carefully stir in extra virgin olive oil.

<u>**Step Two**</u>

1 bunch asparagus, tough ends removed
1 teaspoon salt
2 tablespoons shredded Parmigiano-Reggiano

Wash asparagus. If using large asparagus, peel each stalk with a vegetable peeler. If using small asparagus, do not peel. Fill a pot with water and add salt. Bring to a boil. Add asparagus and blanch one minute, or until tender, but still firm. Drain.

Using tongs, plate asparagus. Drizzle a small amount of balsamic vinegar from step one on asparagus. Top with Parmesan to taste.

Recommended Wine
Rabbit Ridge Sauvignon blanc, Chardonnay

During the growing season, strong tendrils and leaves reach toward the light.

Braised Artichoke Hearts

Erich and I were served these wonderful braised artichoke hearts in our room on an antipasti dish in Maui. Serve these alone or place them on toasted bread for Crostini.

Step One

Serves 2

**2 - 4 medium artichokes, ½ inch of stem
and leaf tip cut off, washed**
2 cups low-salt chicken stock
1 teaspoon salt

Place whole artichoke in a large pot with chicken stock. Add enough water to cover by 1 inch. Add salt. Bring to a boil. Lower heat and simmer 30 minutes, or until leaves pull away easily. Remove all the leaves and serve with the hearts, or save for another use. Scrape out the hairy choke in the center, above the heart. Trim outside of heart and stem, and cut in half.

Step Two

1 tablespoon extra virgin olive oil
Salt and pepper to taste

Drizzle with a touch of extra virgin olive oil and sauté for 5 minutes until lightly browned and tender. Add salt and pepper to taste. Serve warm.

Braised Romaine with Demi-Glace

This is my version of a vegetable dish I tried at an Italian restaurant in Florida. Make or buy high quality demi-glace.

Step One - **Make Roasted Garlic Cloves**

1 whole garlic bulb, outer papery skin removed
1 tablespoon extra virgin olive oil

Step Two

1 tablespoon unsalted butter
½ cup demi-glace
Roasted garlic cloves, from step 1, cut in half, lengthwise

Step Three

½ teaspoon arrowroot
1 teaspoon soy sauce

Step Four

2-4 small heads romaine lettuce, quartered
Salted water

Serves 2

Place garlic bulb in foil. Drizzle with 1-tablespoon extra virgin olive oil. Close foil tightly. Roast in 350º oven 40 minutes. Cool. Peel skin from individual cloves. Reserve for step 2.

Melt butter. Add demi-glace and roasted garlic cloves and bring to a simmer. Reduce by half. Keep warm.

Combine arrowroot and soy sauce. Add to demi-glace. Boil until thickened.

Wash lettuce. Trim tips ½ inch. Make sure to keep the head intact at the end. Place in salted, boiling water. Blanch until tender, about 1 minute. Carefully lift out of water and quickly drain on a paper towel. Place romaine on a plate and lightly brush with demi-glace, coating all sides. Drizzle with more demi-glace and top with garlic.

Recommended Wine
Rabbit Ridge Pinot noir, Merlot, Cabernet Sauvignon

As the vines flourish on the wire, the leaves become so full that they shade the grape clusters from the sun. Periodically, the leaves are pulled by hand from the vines for better sun contact.

Caramelized Brussels Sprouts

I tasted a dish like this in Ohio, while visiting our good friends and wine distributor, Vintner Select. I never would have imagined how good Brussels sprouts could be until I tasted these.

Step One

3 cups Brussels sprouts
1 pinch of salt

Step Two

1 –2 tablespoon unsalted butter

Step Three

½ cup low-sodium chicken stock or beef
** bouillon**
1 teaspoon honey
Ground pepper and salt to taste

Serves 2

Rinse, drain and trim the very end of each Brussels sprout. Fill a medium sized pot with enough water to cover brussels sprouts. Add salt. Bring to a boil. Drop in Brussels sprouts, and blanch for 5 minutes. Do not overcook or they will turn brown. Drain and run under cold water to stop the cooking process. Drain again.

Cut each Brussels sprout in half, lengthwise. Melt butter in a large, flat griddle or sauté pan with a flat bottom. Turn up the heat to medium-high and place each brussels sprout half, cut side down, on the griddle. Do not move until well browned. Sear, until caramelized, but not burned. Turn to the other side, and brown.

When both sides are nicely browned, pour chicken stock, or bouillon over brussels sprouts. Stir constantly to deglaze the pan. Sauté 5 minutes or until all the liquid has evaporated. Drizzle honey over brussels sprouts and warm 1 minute. Season with pepper and salt if needed. Serve warm.

Recommended Wine
Rabbit Ridge Viognier, Chardonnay, Sauvignon blanc

Caramelized Onions

This is a great topping for grilled meats.

Step One

2 large red onions, cut in half lengthwise

Step Two

1 tablespoon extra virgin olive oil
1 tablespoon white or balsamic vinegar
1 teaspoon Rabbit Ridge Sangiovese, or other red wine
½ teaspoon of brown sugar
½ teaspoon fresh thyme leaves
Salt and pepper to taste

Serves 2-4

Peel and slice onions.

Place extra virgin olive oil in a cold sauté pan. Turn on stove to medium-high. When olive oil begins to shimmer, add onions and sauté 2 minutes. Add vinegar, wine, sugar, thyme, salt and pepper. Cook, stirring frequently, until all liquid is absorbed and the onions are caramelized and brown. If onions become dry, deglaze with more red wine.

Recommended Wine
Rabbit Ridge Merlot, Sangiovese

Grilled Peppers

This is a great side dish or appetizer for my antipasti dish on page 8.

<u>*Step One*</u>

<u>*Serves 2*</u>

2 red peppers
2 yellow peppers
2 green peppers

Wash peppers and cut into large chunks. Remove seeds and white membrane.

<u>*Step Two*</u>

1 clove fresh garlic, minced
1 tablespoons extra virgin olive oil
1 tablespoon balsamic vinegar
1 tablespoon fresh basil, minced
1 tablespoon fresh parsley, minced

Combine garlic, oil, vinegar and seasonings in a zip-lock baggie. Marinate pepper chunks in mixture for at least 2 hours. Remove peppers from marinade and let drain 1 minute. Grill peppers, skin side down, or broil, skin side up, until tender and roasted. Serve with poultry, on bruschetta, or as a side vegetable.

Recommended Wine
Rabbit Ridge Pinot noir, Zinfandel

Grilled Zucchini, Summer, or Patty Pan Squash

This is a very simple, pure recipe for squash. Grilling allows the natural sweetness to come out without adding any additional ingredients. Just before serving, a simple drizzle of high quality extra virgin olive oil and salt and pepper is all that is needed.

Step One

4 zucchini or summer squash, or 8 patty pan squash, washed, peeled and ends trimmed

Step Two

1 tablespoon high quality extra virgin olive oil

Salt and pepper to taste

Balsamic vinegar (optional)

Serves 4

Slice squash into 1/4 inch slices. Set aside. Season squash with salt and pepper. Heat grill to high. Spray racks with non-stick spray. Place squash on grill racks and sear. Do not move squash until grill lines are present. Turn once to mark the other side. Do not overcook.

Remove squash to plates, drizzle with olive oil. Season with salt and pepper and serve hot. If desired, drizzle with Balsamic vinegar.

Recommended Wine
Rabbit Ridge Chardonnay

Roasted Garlic Mashed Potatoes

These potatoes have great flavor. It is very important to keep all of the ingredients warm before combining. Adjust the garlic to your own taste.

<u>**Step One**</u>   <u>*Serves 4-6*</u>

Roasted garlic cloves, from page 35   Put garlic in a mini processor and puree as
2 tablespoons milk   finely as possible. Add milk and puree into
                                                                     a smooth paste. Set aside.

<u>**Step Two**</u>

4 large baking potatoes   Peel potatoes and cut into large pieces.
Water   Place potatoes and salt in a pan and add
Salt to taste   enough water to cover by 1 inch. Bring to
                                                                     a boil. Lower heat and simmer until pota-
                                                                     toes are tender, about 20 minutes. Drain
                                                                     and keep warm.

<u>**Step Three**</u>

½ cup milk or cream   Warm milk or cream, and sour cream. Add
2 tablespoon sour cream   1 tablespoon garlic puree from step 1. Mash
4 tablespoon butter   or whisk potatoes with as much milk mix-
Salt and pepper to taste   ture and butter as needed. Add salt and
                                                                     pepper to taste. Add more garlic if desired.

<u>Recommended Wine</u>
Rabbit Ridge Chardonnay

Sautéed Broccoli with Garlic

I prepare this recipe more than any other. I like to get the garlic and broccoli well browned but still firm. Mixing cauliflower with the broccoli is also fun.

Step One

8 cloves garlic, cut in thick slivers
2 tablespoons extra virgin olive oil
1 large head broccoli, cleaned and
   florets separated
1 teaspoon soy sauce
Salt and pepper to taste

Serves 2

In a large sauté pan, sauté garlic in olive oil 5 minutes. Turn off heat and let sit 30 minutes. Add broccoli and sauté over medium-low heat, stirring frequently until broccoli is tender, about 30 minutes. Do not burn garlic. Do not overcook. Add soy sauce and salt and pepper. Cook 1 minute. Serve hot.

Recommended Wine
Rabbit Ridge Viognier, Chardonnay

A vegetable stand in Lecci, the Chianti region of Tuscany in Italy.

Fresh vegetables are the foundation of most dishes. These tomatoes, onions, peppers and garlic will form the base of my chili.

Sautéed Leeks

This is nice with any main course.

Step One

Serves 2-4

2 - 4 bunches leeks, white part and 2 inches green, cut in half lengthwise and washed

1 tablespoon butter

½ cup chicken stock

Pinch of sugar

Salt and pepper to taste

Slice leeks into 1/4 inch pieces. Heat butter in a sauté pan. Add leeks, stock, sugar, salt and pepper. Sauté leeks, stirring frequently, until tender and liquid is reduced to syrup.

Recommended Wine
Rabbit Ridge Chardonnay

Sautéed Mushrooms

I continue to come up with different versions for sautéed mushrooms, possibly because they are so versatile and pair well with many seasonings. They are great on top of steaks. I love them on for crostini, served as an appetizer.

Step 1

Serves 2

1 tablespoon butter

3 cups assorted fresh mushrooms, wiped clean, sliced

Salt and pepper to taste

1 teaspoon Worcestershire sauce

1/8 cup Rabbit Ridge Chardonnay

1/8 cup beef or vegetable stock

2 cloves fresh garlic, minced

1 tablespoon minced parsley

Extra virgin olive oil (optional)

Melt butter. Add mushrooms, salt and pepper. Sauté until all liquid is absorbed. Add Worchester, wine, beef stock, and garlic. Continue cooking until mushrooms are browned and liquid has evaporated. Serve warm. Top with parsley.

For Crostini, toast bread rounds, spread mushroom mixture on top and drizzle with olive oil. Make sure there is no liquid left.

Recommended Wine

Rabbit Ridge Chardonnay, Pinot noir

Sautéed Spinach

Erich and I love this spinach preparation. I like to start step one very early so that the garlic flavor can intensify.

Step One

8 cloves fresh garlic, sliced thick length-wise

1 tablespoon extra virgin olive oil

Step Two

4 cups fresh spinach, washed and stemmed.

2 cloves fresh garlic, chopped fine

½ teaspoon soy sauce (optional)

Salt and pepper to taste

Lemon wedges (optional)

Serves 2

In a large sauté pan, sauté garlic in oil on low heat for 5 minutes. Do not burn. Turn off heat and let sit for up to two hours.

Add spinach, uncooked garlic, and soy sauce to pan with cooked garlic. Sauté until spinach is just wilted, about 3 minutes. Do not overcook. Season with salt and pepper. Serve hot with a squeeze of fresh lemon, if desired.

Recommended Wine

Rabbit Ridge Chardonnay, Pinot noir, Sauvignon blanc

The San Marcos Road, Cristalla Ranch Vineyard is 8 years old. It has 11 varieties of grapes planted on it. Varieties include: Cabernet Sauvignon, Canernet Franc, Primitivo, Petit Verdot, Refosco, Petite Sirah, Syrah, Sauvignon blanc, Sangiovese, Vernaccia and Zinfandel.

Sautéed Sunchokes with Olive Oil and Rosemary

Sunchokes are the bulb of the sunflower plant, also called Jerusalem artichokes. They are carried in the vegetable section of most supermarkets these days. Peel the sunchokes like you would a potato. It is a little tricky because they are small, but well worth the effort.

Step One

1 package sunchokes
1 teaspoon extra virgin olive oil
1 teaspoon fresh rosemary, minced
Salt and pepper to taste

Serves 2

Peel sunchokes. Slice ¼ inch thick. Warm olive oil in a non-stick pan. Place sunchokes, rosemary, salt, and pepper in a pan and sauté until chokes are brown and cooked through. Serve warm.

Recommended Wine
Rabbit Ridge Cabernet Sauvignon, Zinfandel

Southern Tamale

This is an adaptation of one of my mother's recipes. The original recipe uses canned corn, however when in season, fresh is always best. Using a food processor will make this dish very quick.

<u>**Step One**</u>

4 ears fresh corn
½ teaspoon low-fat milk or cream
1 pinch of nutmeg

<u>**Step Two**</u>

1 cup tomato, seeded and diced
¼ cup onion, minced
½ cup green pepper, white membrane removed and cut into small dice
Salt and pepper to taste
2 strips of bacon

<u>*Serves 4*</u>

Boil or microwave corn in water for 5 minutes. Drain. Cut corn off the cob. Divide corn in half. Roughly puree ½ of the corn with the cream. Combine pureed corn with whole kernal corn and nutmeg in a saucepan and bring to a simmer. Cook 2 minutes on medium-low. Set aside for step 2.

Pre-heat over to 350º. Grease a casserole dish. Put ½ of corn on the bottom. Evenly top with ½ of the tomato, ½ of the onion and ½ of the green pepper. Salt and generously pepper first layer. Spread remaining cup of corn and vegetables in the same order as the first layer. Add more pepper. Place bacon strips on top and bake at 350º for 30-45 minutes or until bacon is browned. Serve hot.

<u>**Recommended Wine**</u>
Rabbit Ridge Sauvignon blanc, Chardonnay, Viognier

Spaghetti Squash with Garlic and Parmesan

I used to eat this dish every time I visited one of my neighborhood Italian restaurants in Florida. I tried to make this a bit lighter than the buttery version prepared by the chef. If you really want to go crazy, add more butter.

Step One

Serves 4

1 small spaghetti squash

Pre-heat oven to 350º. Cut squash in half, lengthwise. Scrape out the seeds with a spoon. Place on a cookie sheet and bake 1 hour. Cool. Remove strands of spaghetti from the skin using a fork. Place squash in a casserole dish lightly sprayed with pam.

Step Two

1 tablespoons unsalted butter
2 tablespoons extra virgin olive oil
8 cloves garlic, sliced
2 tablespoons fresh parsley, minced
¼ cup grated Parmigiano-Reggiano
Salt and pepper to taste

Sauté garlic in butter and oil 5 minutes. Add to squash. Stir. Add salt, pepper, parsley and parmesan and mix thoroughly. Bake 15 minutes at 350º. Just before serving, drizzle with a bit more extra virgin olive oil.

Recommended Wine
Rabbit Ridge Chardonnay

Zucchini or Summer Squash sautéed with Herbs

This is a quick and light vegetable side dish. Look for small, firm zucchini or summer squash.

<u>**Step One**</u>   <u>*Serves 4*</u>

4 medium squash or zucchini
1 tablespoon extra virgin olive oil
1 tablespoon butter
1 medium yellow onion, finely diced
¼ teaspoon fresh thyme, minced
½ teaspoon fresh basil, minced
Salt and pepper to taste

Wash squash. Peel every other strip. Cut julienne 1/8 inch slices or in rounds. Sauté onion in butter and extra virgin olive oil for 2 minutes. Add squash, thyme, basil, salt and pepper and sauté until cooked through and lightly browned. Do not cover. Do not over cook.

<u>*Version Two*</u>

<u>**Step One**</u>

1 tablespoon extra virgin olive oil
1 tablespoon butter
2 large shallots, peeled and sliced
¼ teaspoon fresh thyme, minced
¼ teaspoon fresh basil, minced
Salt and pepper to taste

Warm extra virgin olive oil and butter. Add shallots. Sauté until lightly brown, do not burn. Remove from heat and stir in seasonings.

Fill a pot large enough to hold squash. Add salt and bring to a boil. Blanch squash in water for 2 minutes. Squash should still be under-cooked. Drain and place in cold water to stop the cooking process. Drain again. Toss squash into shallot and thyme mixture from step 1. Sauté until lightly browned and cooked through.

<u>**Step Two**</u>

4 squash or zucchini, cleaned and sliced

<u>Recommended Wine</u>
Rabbit Ridge Chardonnay

In early summer, new buds form on the vine. This is the beginning of the seasons grape crop.

BUD BREAK and SOUPS

Cream of Broccoli Soup, Cauliflower, or Celery   56

Cream of Mushroom Soup   58

Carrot Soup with Fresh Dill and Crème Fraîche   59

Dad's Chili   61

Gazpacho   62

Roasted Red Bell Pepper Soup   68

Split Pea Soup   69

Tomato/Basil Soup and Tomato/Cucumber Soup   73

Vichyssoise   75

Cream of Broccoli Soup, Cauliflower, or Celery

Make sure you buy fresh, dark green broccoli with tight florets and a firm stalk. This soup is great hot or cold. Cauliflower or celery may be used in place of broccoli.

Step One

2 tablespoons unsalted butter
1½ cups yellow onion, chopped

Step Two

2 heads fresh broccoli, cauliflower or celery
1¼ qt. chicken stock (low sodium)
1/8 cup chardonnay
½ teaspoon white pepper

Step Three

1 teaspoon dried sweet basil, or chervil
¼ cup heavy cream or low fat cream (optional)
Salt to taste

An original stone sink at the home in Lecci, Italy. My simple celery soup was great using fresh local produce.

Serves 8

Sauté onion in butter on low heat until soft but not brown.

Clean, and separate broccoli florets. Add to the pan with the onions. Add stock, wine and white pepper and bring to a boil. Reduce heat to medium low and simmer 30 minutes. Cool slightly. Puree in a blender. Strain through a mesh colander, if using celery.

Return soup to pan and stir in remaining ingredients. Warm a few minutes. Do not boil. Serve hot or cold.

Recommended Wine
Rabbit Ridge Chardonnay

Close-up view of new growth shows bud hair, which protects the plant from excessive water loss.

Cream of Mushroom Soup

This is another simple soup recipe. Mixing mushroom varieties gives this soup even more interest.

Step One

5 cups fresh mushrooms

Serves 4

Trim stems from mushrooms. Clean mushrooms with a damp paper towel. Thickly slice all mushrooms. Sct aside.

Step Two

2 tablespoons unsalted butter
1 cup mixed shallots and yellow onions, sliced
3 fresh thyme sprigs, tied together
4 cups chicken stock (low sodium)

Melt butter in a medium stockpot. Add onions and shallots and sauté 5 minutes on low heat. Add thyme and mushrooms and sauté 5 minutes or until tender. Add chicken stock and bring to a boil. Reduce heat to low and simmer 20 minutes. Cool slightly. Remove thyme sprigs. Puree in a blender. Pour back into the pan.

Step Three

¼ to ½ cup heavy cream
2 tablespoons sherry (optional)
Salt and pepper to taste

Add cream, sherry, salt and pepper to pan. Whisk. Warm, but do not boil. Adjust seasoning and serve.

Recommended Wine
Rabbit Ridge Chardonnay

Carrot Soup with Fresh Dill and Crème Fraiché

Use only very fresh, firm carrots. If using organic carrots, there is no need to peel. Simply rub off the skins with a scouring sponge.

<u>*Step One*</u> - **Make Crème Fraiché -**
 or purchase ready-made

1 cup sour cream

1 cup heavy whipping cream

1 pinch sugar

<u>*Step Two*</u>

3 tablespoons butter

2 small shallots, minced

2 small leaks, white part and 1 inch of
  green, washed and chopped fine

3½ cups carrots, peeled and coarsely
  chopped

1 quart chicken stock, low sodium

1 teaspoon white pepper

½ teaspoon grated orange rind

Salt to taste

<u>*Step Three*</u>

¼ - ½ cup crème fraîche, from above

1/8 **cup fresh dill, chopped**

Serves 4

Whisk all ingredients. Pour in a glass container and cover with plastic wrap. Place in a warm spot for 8 hours. Stir, and then place in the refrigerator overnight until ready to use.

Melt butter on medium heat. Add shallots and leeks. Sauté 5 minutes. Add carrots, stock, and pepper and bring to a boil. Reduce to low. Simmer for 1 hour, partially covered. Add orange rind and warm 3 minutes. Cool slightly. Puree in a blender. Strain into a clean pan. Add salt to taste.

Place soup into soup bowls. Spoon a dollop of crème fraîche in the middle of the carrot soup or stir in completely for a creamier soup. Add more stock if needed. Garnish with dill. Serve hot or cold.

| <u>**Recommended Wine**</u> |
| Rabbit Ridge Chardonnay |

Young shoots are visible on bright green foliage.

Grape clusters develop from the tiny buds.

Healthy bud formation is crucial for good grape quality.

Dad's Chili

My dad, Bill James, gave this recipe to me. This was the first recipe my father prepared after he retired as a bank president in 1984. Dad's chili continues to be a family favorite.

Step One

1 pound ground beef or turkey

Step Two

1 tablespoon extra virgin olive oil

1 cup onion, coarsely chopped

1 cup green pepper, coarsely chopped

2 cloves garlic, minced

Step Three

1 can (28 oz.) chopped tomatoes with juice

1 can (8 oz.) tomato sauce

1 can (15½ oz.) kidney beans (optional)

¼ cup Rabbit Ridge Merlot

1 tablespoon chili powder

1 tablespoon garlic powder

2 tablespoons worcestershire sauce

1 teaspoon oregano

1 teaspoon cumin

1 teaspoon red wine vinegar

¼ teaspoon paprika

Cayenne pepper to taste

Salt to taste

Step Four

Shredded Cheddar cheese (optional)

2 green onions, sliced thin (optional)

Tabasco (optional)

Serves 8

Brown meat in a large pot. Drain in a colander to remove fat. Place meat in a bowl and set aside.

Add olive oil and vegetables to pan and sauté 5 minutes. Do not burn garlic. Return browned meat to pan with vegetables.

Add remaining ingredients and bring to a boil. Reduce heat and simmer 45 minutes. Add more red wine or water if chili becomes too thick.

Top chili with cheese, green onions, or Tabasco, if desired.

Recommended Wine
Rabbit Ridge Merlot, Zinfandel, Syrah, Cabernet Sauvignon

Gazpacho

This is another very low-fat and flavorful soup. Gazpacho is great on a warm day. Make sure your peppers are very firm and fresh. If you prefer a smoother soup, the mixture can be purèed. We like it very chunky.

Step One

2 cloves garlic

½ green bell pepper

½ red bell pepper

½ yellow bell pepper

½ cucumber, peeled and seeded

6 large plum tomatoes, seeded

Serves 8

Place garlic in a processor and finely mince. Add remaining ingredients and finely chop or purèe to desired consistency. Pour into a plastic bowl with a fitted cover.

Step Two

¼ cup red onion, finely chopped

1/8 cup extra virgin olive oil

½ cup Campbell's Beef Consumé

½ cup clamato juice

Juice of 1 lemon

2 tablespoons red wine vinegar

1 teaspoon garlic powder

6 fresh basil leaves, julienned

Salt and pepper to taste

Stir all ingredients into Step One mixture.

Step Three

½ green bell pepper

½ red bell pepper

½ yellow bell pepper

½ large cucumber, peeled and seeded

Finely cut vegetables into even-sized small dice. Stir into soup. Cover and chill.

Step Four

2 green onions, sliced

Tabasco, if desired

Place soup in bowls. Garnish with green onions. Add Tabasco if desired.

Recommended Wine

Rabbit Ridge Sauvignon Blanc

Fragile tendrils develop just below the bud. As the vine develops, the tendrils attach the shoot to the vineyard wire and continue growing and expanding on a vertical plane.

Buds appear as miniature grapes.

Roasted Red Bell Pepper Soup

This is a very tasty and colorful soup. Using very red, firm peppers insures a rich pepper taste. This also makes a wonderful sauce for fish.

Step One
3 - 4 large red bell peppers, washed

Step Two
1 tablespoon butter

1 cup yellow onion, finely chopped

1 - 2 cups chicken stock

Salt and pepper to taste

Serves 4

Pre-heat broiler or gas stove. Place peppers on foil and broil until charred completely black on all sides; or char on the stove. Place peppers in a paper bag to steam for a few minutes. Discard charred skin. Clean out seeds and white membrane. Chop peppers roughly.

Melt butter. Add onion and sauté 2 minutes. Add peppers and chicken stock. Simmer 30 minutes partially covered. Cool slightly. Puree in blender. Add salt and pepper.

For Red Pepper sauce: Add 2 cloves of garlic, cut in half to step two. Remove garlic before pureeing. Reduce stock to sauce consistency. Add a tiny bit of lemon juice and balsamic just before serving. Serve with grilled or baked white fish.

Recommended Wine
Rabbit Ridge Chardonnay

Split Pea Soup

This is a meal in itself. We love this soup because it is so healthy and satisfying.

Serves 8

Step One

1 package (16 ounces) green or yellow split peas

Rinse peas. Place in a large pot.

Step Two

2 carrots, cut in large chunks

2 celery stalks, cut in large chunks

1 medium onion, chopped

1 clove garlic

Place all vegetables in a food processor and process until well chopped. Place vegetables in the pot with the split peas.

Step Three

1 quart chicken or vegetable stock (low salt)

Water

1 teaspoon dried basil

Pepper to taste

Salt to taste

Pour stock over peas and vegetables. Add enough water to cover peas by 2 inches. Add basil and pepper. Stir. Bring to a boil. Reduce heat to simmer and cook until peas are tender. Stir frequently. Add water as needed. Add salt at the end of cooking, if needed.

Recommended Wine

Rabbit Ridge Chardonnay

"Verasion" is the first show of color on the grape berries.

During verasion, the sugar level in the berries increases and the acidity decreases.

Tomato/Basil Soup

Canned tomatoes can be used if fresh tomatoes are out of season. Just make sure to use a high quality brand without a lot of salt.

Step One

2 tablespoons unsalted butter

1 large carrot

1 celery stalk

1 medium onion

2 cloves garlic

Step Two

2-3 pounds fresh tomatoes or 32 oz. whole canned tomatoes

3 cups unsalted chicken stock

1 tablespoon double-concentrated tomato paste

8 large fresh basil leaves, roughly torn

White pepper to taste

¼ cup Rabbit Ridge Chardonnay

¼ teaspoon sugar

Step Three

10 large fresh basil leaves, finely julienne (chiffonade)

Salt to taste

1 cup heavy cream (optional)

Serves 2

Melt butter in a soup pot. Finely chop vegetables in a processor. Place vegetables in the soup pot with hot butter and sauté on medium high heat for 5 minutes.

Coarsely chop tomatoes. Add tomatoes and their juices to the pan. Add chicken stock, tomato paste, basil, pepper and sugar. Simmer on low for 30 minutes, stirring frequently. Cool slightly. Puree in a blender in batches. Strain into a clean pan (straining will remove the seeds).

Stir in basil and salt. Serve warm or cold. If desired, add cream, stir and serve.

Tomato/Cucumber Soup

Follow steps one and two above. Omit step three above. Add cucumber juice to tomato soup.

2 large cucumbers, peeled

Salt and pepper to taste

Juice cucumbers in a juice machine or puree in a blender. If pureeing, strain. Add to soup. Adjust seasoning and chill.

Recommended Wine

Sauvignon blanc or Chardonnay

As the berries reach the "final swell" stage, they will begin to soften. Red grapes will begin to change from green to purple. White grapes will change from green to yellow.

Weather will affect how quickly the berries ripen. Warm summers will speed up the ripening process and cool weather will slow the process down.

Vichyssoise

I love vichyssoise, but I hate the guilt. I have tried to make this lighter by decreasing the cream and butter and increasing the leeks. I recommend putting this soup in the freezer 30 minutes prior to serving to really chill it.

Step One

Serves 8

2 cups chopped leeks, use only the white part and 1 inch of the green

3 tablespoons unsalted butter

4 cups potatoes, peeled and sliced

32 ounces chicken stock

1 tablespoon white pepper

Sauté leeks in butter for 5 minutes. Add potatoes, stock and white pepper. Simmer on medium-low for 45 minutes. Cool slightly. Puree in batches. Return to pan.

Step Two

1 pint low-fat milk

1 cup heavy cream or low fat half and half

Salt to taste

Add milk and cream and whisk. Season to taste with salt. Chill until very cold.

Recommended Wine
Rabbit Ridge Chardonnay

HARVEST TIME and PASTA/RICE/BEANS

Black Beans

A Spanish friend I worked with in Tampa, Florida, gave me this recipe. Just before serving, I like to top the beans with fresh onion, extra virgin olive oil, and vinegar for added layering and depth of flavor.

Step One

Serves 8

1 bag black beans

Rinse the beans. Place in a large bowl and cover with at least 4 inches of water. Place in the refrigerator 8 hours. Change water twice during the 8 hours.

Step Two

3 tablespoons extra virgin olive oil
1 large green pepper, chopped
1 large onion, chopped
5 cloves fresh garlic, minced
2 bay leaves
1 Knorr chicken bouillon cube

Sauté green pepper, onion and garlic in extra virgin olive oil 5 minutes. Drain beans and add to pot with bay leaves. Cover with water by 4 inches. Add bouillon cube. Cook 2 - 4 hours, or until tender. Cover partially, stir often and add water as needed.

Step Three

2 tablespoons extra virgin olive oil
1 tablespoon red wine vinegar
Pinch of sugar
white or yellow rice
  (optional)
1 small red onion, chopped fine
 Tabasco to taste (optional)

Just before serving, add extra virgin olive oil, vinegar and sugar. Adjust salt if needed Serve in a bowl, with or without rice, top with onions and Tabasco, if desired.

Recommended Wine
Rabbit Ridge Merlot, Barbera, Primitivo

Brown Rice with Leeks and Cranberries

I created this rice dish for Thanksgiving. Since Erich doesn't care for sweet potatoes, I make him rice or mashed potatoes instead.

<u>**Step One**</u>   <u>*Serves 2-4*</u>

1 cup brown rice (not instant)   Sauté leeks in butter until soft. Add rice
½ cup chopped leeks, white part only and warm.
1 tablespoon butter

<u>**Step Two**</u>

1 cup chicken stock   Add stock and water to rice and bring to a
1 cup water   boil. Cover and simmer on medium-low
½ cup dried cranberries   for 45 minutes. Cook until tender. Add more
Salt and pepper to taste   water if needed. When almost all liquid is
                                      absorbed, add cranberries, salt and pepper
                                      and warm 5 minutes.

Recommended Wine
Rabbit Ridge Pinot noir, Merlot

Erich and Joanne Russell walk through the Cristalla Vineyard sampling grape sugars. The level of sugar, or "brix" will indicate when the grapes are ready to pick. Sampling for sugars is done by taking random samples of berries from each varietal. The berries are crushed by hand and tested for approximate sugar levels, using a refractometer. (This is usually done out in the field). The decision to harvest is determined by three things: Sugar has to be high enough, acid must not be too low, and the varietal flavor must be at its optimum. Erich can tell by taste if the grapes are ready.

Linguini with Clam Sauce

There is nothing better than buttery clams with linguini. I also use this recipe for steamed clams or mussels.

<hr>

Step One

2 pounds fresh cherrystone clams

Step Two

2 tablespoons extra virgin olive oil

1 tablespoon unsalted butter

4 cloves garlic, chopped fine

¼ cup onion, finely chopped

Pinch red pepper flakes

2 cans whole baby or chopped clams drained, juice reserved

¼ cup Chardonnay

Fresh clams from step one

1 tablespoon fresh parsley, chopped

Salt and pepper to taste

Step Three

8 ounces linguine

Serves 2

Wash clams in a colander. Place in a plastic bowl and cover with cold water. Soak for a couple of hours. Drain and rinse well.

In a clean medium pan, sauté garlic and onion in extra virgin olive oil and butter for 2 minutes. Do not burn. Add red pepper flakes and warm. Add clam juice from step 2 canned clams, and wine to pan. Boil one minute. Place fresh clams in pan, cover, and steam until clams open. Remove clams and set aside. Keep warm. Discard any clams that did not open. Strain liquid through a paper towel lined strainer. Return liquid to pan. Boil for 2 minutes. Stir in canned clams, parsley, salt and pepper. Adjust seasonings. Add more butter if desired.

Cook pasta according to package directions. Drain and toss with a touch of extra virgin olive oil. Toss with clam sauce. Place pasta on plates and top with fresh clams from step 1. Serve hot.

Recommended Wine
Rabbit Ridge Chardonnay

Orzo with Fresh Herbs

My sister, Kathy and I always have fresh herbs growing in the garden. This side dish is a wonderful way to enjoy a variety of herbs in season. Orzo is cooked just like pasta so it can be prepared ahead of time. For a formal dinner, press cooked orzo mixture into a mold or ramekin; warm, then unmold onto plates at serving time.

Step One

½ box orzo
2 - 3 cups chicken stock
Water
1 tablespoon butter

Step Two

½ cup assorted fresh herbs, chopped
  such as: dill, basil, parsley, tarragon
Salt and pepper to taste

Serves 6

Cook orzo, following package directions in chicken stock, and as much water needed to cover by 2 inches. Drain orzo and reserve ½ cup of cooking liquid. Place orzo back in pan and stir in butter. Add a touch of cooking liquid to moisten, if needed.

Stir in herbs, salt and pepper. Serve warm.

Fresh tarragon grows like a weed in our California herb garden.

Recommended Wine
Rabbit Ridge Chardonnay

Paella

This Paella dish is wonderfully light. I like the nuttiness of natural brown rice paired with saffron and shrimp. Paella takes a bit of effort to make, but it is well worth the time involved.

<u>Step One</u>

1 cup brown rice

2 ½ cups water

½ teaspoon salt

<u>Step Two</u>

2 tablespoons extra virgin olive oil

½ cup onion, diced

2 garlic cloves, minced

½ red pepper, cleaned and diced

½ green pepper, cleaned and diced

1 teaspoon saffron

¼ cup Rabbit Ridge Chardonnay

Pinch of sugar

½ teaspoon garlic powder

Salt and cayenne pepper to taste

½ cup raw shrimp, peeled and de-veined

2 tablespoons fresh parsley, minced

1 tomato, seeded and chopped

<u>Step Three</u>

½ cup cooked turkey or chicken sausage (traditional chorizo can be used)

1 cup frozen peas, thawed

<u>Step Four</u>

¼ cup clam juice

1 dozen fresh clams, washed

<u>Serves 8</u>

Cook rice in salted water until al dente (Slightly underdone). Set aside.

Place extra virgin olive oil in a medium sized pan. Add onion, garlic, and peppers and sauté until tender. Do not over cook. Add saffron, wine, sugar and seasonings. Sauté 2 minutes. Add shrimp and sauté until barely cooked. Stir in rice, parsley and tomato.

Slice sausage into 1-inch rounds. Stir sausage and peas into rice mixture. Place in a paella pan or casserole dish

Pre-heat oven to 325º. Place clam juice in a medium sized pan on the stove. Place clams in the pan and steam on medium-high heat until clams open. Immediately remove clams from pan with tongs. Set clams aside. Strain clam juice and add to rice mixture. Gently stir all ingredients, except clams, set aside. Place rice mixture in the oven and warm for 20 minutes. Place clams in their shells on top of the rice and warm another 5 minutes. Serve hot.

<u>Recommended Wine</u>
Rabbit Ridge Chardonnay

Pasta with Mushroom Sauce

I love mushrooms and today it is quite easy to find exotic varieties. I have been perfecting this sauce for years. This mixture can also be placed on bread rounds for costini before a meal.

Step One

Serves 4

2 tablespoons butter

1 tablespoon extra virgin olive oil

2 tablespoons minced shallots

3 cups shitake, button or combination of assorted mushrooms, sliced

3- 4 tablespoons sherry

¾ cup to 1 cup beef stock

½ cup heavy cream or low fat milk

1 teaspoon chervil

Salt and pepper to taste

Sauté shallots in butter and olive oil. Add mushrooms and sauté until brown. Add sherry and beef stock. Simmer until thickened. Add cream, chervil, salt and pepper. Warm 1 minute.

Cook pasta according to package directions. Toss with sauce and parsley. Serve with cheese.

Step Two

16 ounces pasta

½ cup Parmigiano-Reggiano

1 tablespoon minced parsley

Recommended Wine
Rabbit Ridge Chardonnay

Pasta with Bolognese

There are many recipes for bolognese sauce. The traditional Bolognese sauce from Bologna, Italy, uses milk in the sauce. I prefer to leave the milk out and focus on a very meaty sauce with just a hint of tomato.

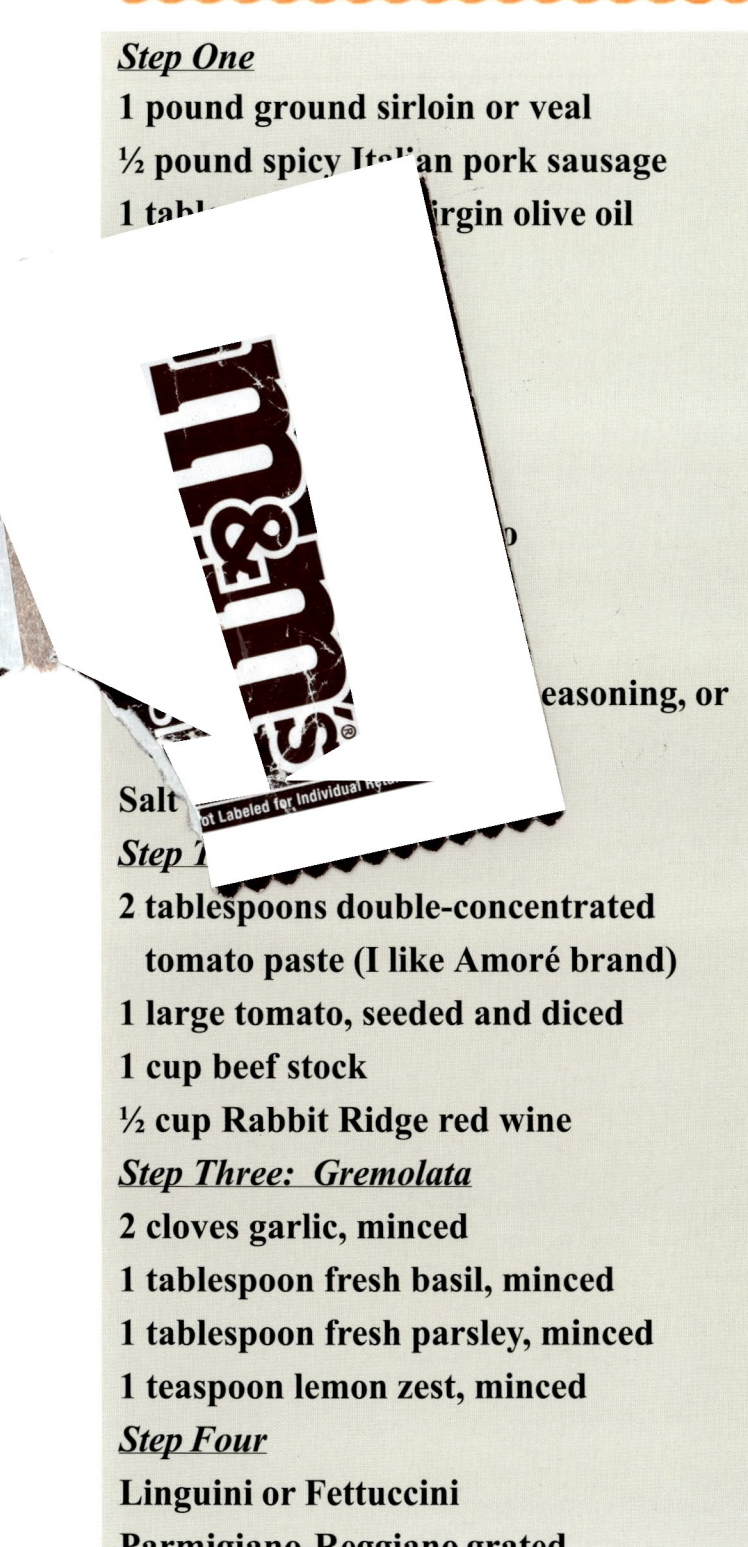

Step One

1 pound ground sirloin or veal

½ pound spicy Italian pork sausage

1 tablespoon extra virgin olive oil

Serves 8

Place extra virgin olive oil, meat and pork in a stockpot. Finely chop remaining 4 vegetables in a food processor. Add to pot. Cook on medium heat, stirring often until meat is completely cooked and vegetables are soft. Stir in seasonings. Cook 2 minutes.

...easoning, or

Salt

Step Two

2 tablespoons double-concentrated tomato paste (I like Amoré brand)

1 large tomato, seeded and diced

1 cup beef stock

½ cup Rabbit Ridge red wine

Stir in tomato paste, tomato, stock and wine. Bring to a boil. Cover partially, and simmer on low for 45 minutes, stirring frequently.

Step Three: Gremolata

2 cloves garlic, minced

1 tablespoon fresh basil, minced

1 tablespoon fresh parsley, minced

1 teaspoon lemon zest, minced

Combine ingredients. Set-aside until ready to serve.

Step Four

Linguini or Fettuccini

Parmigiano-Reggiano grated

Cook pasta according to package directions. Drain. Toss with half of the sauce. Place on plates. Top with more sauce, parmesan and a small amount of gremolata to taste.

Recommended Wine
Rabbit Ridge Syrah, Zinfandel, Merlot, Dolcetto or Primitivo

Mature Refosco grapes have a sugar between 22 and 24 brix. To calculate the alcohol, multiply .55 by the brix figure. This will equal the alcohol percentage. For example - grapes with a brix of 25.5, would have an alcohol content of 14% (25.5 x .55=14). Grapes picked at too low a brix will taste thin and tart. Grapes picked with too high a brix can actually taste hot. Standard picking brix are: Reds 20-24; Whites 19-23; Blush 19-23; and Sparkling 18-20.

During the picking stage, dramatic changes in the weather, such as rain or frost or even sudden spikes in temperature can greatly decrease the quality of the juice. It is critical to the quality of the wine that harvest be quick.

Dozens of pickers line the vineyard with cutters, bins and tractors. Some pick while others drive the loaded bins of grapes to the crusher.

Pasta with Herbed Marinara

There are a lot of ingredients in this marinara; however, it is very simple to make. For a rich meaty sauce, cooked spicy pork sausage or beef could be added at the end of cooking.

Step One

Serves 4-6

½ cup celery, chopped
1 large yellow onion, chopped
4 cloves fresh garlic, minced
1 cup finely chopped carrot
2 tablespoons extra virgin olive oil
5 large fresh tomatoes, peeled, seeded and chopped
24 oz. canned, chopped tomatoes, drained
1 tablespoon dried thyme
½ teaspoon dried oregano
Pinch of sugar
1 teaspoon dark Worcestershire sauce
1 tablespoon tomato paste
½ cup Chardonnay
Salt and cayenne pepper to taste

Sauté celery, onion, garlic and carrot in extra virgin olive oil until soft. Add remaining ingredients. Simmer 1 hour, partially covered. Stir frequently.

Add basil to sauce. Cook pasta according to package directions. Toss with half of the marinara. Top with more sauce and cheese.

Step Two

½ cup chopped fresh basil
16 ounces pasta
Parmigiano-Reggiano cheese, grated

Recommended Wine
Rabbit Ridge Zinfandel, Syrah or Primitivo

Pearl Barley with Mushrooms

This is my adaptation of a casserole my mother made for us as children. I have added wine and chicken stock to lighten the original buttery version.

Step One

Serves 4-6

½ pound fresh button mushrooms
1 large onion, chopped
3 tablespoons butter

Slice mushroom caps and stems. Cook the onion in butter 3 - 4 minutes. Add mushrooms and sauté for 4 minutes.

Step Two

1 cup pearl barley
2 - 3 cups beef and chicken stock,
   combined and boiling
½ cup Rabbit Ridge Chardonnay
Salt and pepper

Add the barley and cook until lightly browned. Place in a lightly greased casserole and add wine. Add enough stock to cover mixture by ½ inch. Stir in salt and pepper. Cover and bake at 350° for 25 minutes or until barley is done and liquid is absorbed.

Recommended Wine
Rabbit Ridge Chardonnay

Tortellini with Sage

This is a simple pasta dish. In Italy, we were served pasta often with either a sage filling or with sage butter.

Step One

Serves 6

2 tablespoons butter
1 tablespoon extra virgin olive oil
1/8 cup fresh sage, cut in strips
Salt and pepper to taste

Melt butter; add extra virgin olive oil, sage, salt and pepper. Simmer on low until sage is tender. Do not burn the butter.

Step Two

1 package of fresh cheese tortellini
Grated Reggiano parmesan cheese
Pinch of finely minced fresh sage

Bring water to a boil. Cook pasta according to package directions. Drain. Remove half of the sage from the butter with a fork. Toss pasta with the remaining sage butter. Top with parmesan and a pinch of fresh minced sage. Serve hot.

Recommended Wine
Rabbit Ridge Sauvignon blanc, Viognier, Sangiovese, Barbera or Dolcetto

Joanne and Erich Russell inspecting the freshly picked syrah grapes in the Cristalla vineyard. This Syrah will be a reserve wine call Sarah's Syrah, named for Joanne's daughter, Sarah.

CRUSHING THE GRAPES and MEAT ENTRÉES

Grilled Steak

This is a simple steak preparation. It is worth the money to buy Angus or prime beef. Choice beef can be used, just be certain the meat is very red and has some marbling for tenderness.

Step One

2 steaks - Filet, New York Strips, etc.
½ tablespoon garlic powder
Fresh ground pepper to taste
Salt to taste

Serves 2

Combine garlic powder, salt, and pepper. Rub steaks on each side with dry mixture. Bring meat to room temperature. Grill or sauté to desired temperature. Do not overcook.

Stems and grape skins left over from harvest.

Recommended Wine
Rabbit Ridge Cabernet Sauvignon, Syrah, Zinfandel, Merlot

Lamb Chops

These lamb chops are great cooked on the grill. They may be done in the broiler; however, they may smoke and splatter if the marinade drips. If you like, serve these lamb chops with mint jelly.

Step One

2 tablespoon extra virgin olive oil
1 tablespoon fresh garlic, finely minced
1 teaspoon lemon zest, minced
1 tablespoons fresh rosemary, finely minced
1 teaspoon fresh mint, finely minced

Step Two

4 lamb chops
Salt to taste
Pepper to taste
Mint jelly (optional)

Serves 4

Combine all ingredients in a bowl and stir to combine.

Wash, and pat dry lamb. Place in marinade from step one. Turn to coat and refrigerate 1-2 hours.

Assembly: Remove lamb from marinade. Bring lamb to room temperature. Heat grill or broiler. Season lamb with salt and pepper. Grill or broil until cooked to desired temperature. Serve immediately with or without mint jelly.

Recommended Wine
Rabbit Ridge Paso Robles Zinfandel, Primitivo, Merlot, Cabernet Sauvignon

Pot Roast

This is a terrific pot roast. The Pic-a-Peppa sauce adds a wonderful mix of spice and pepper. If you cannot find Pic-a-Peppa sauce, use 1 tablespoon hoisin sauce mixed with 1 teaspoon dark Worchester, 1 teaspoon white wine Worchester and a dash of Tabasco.

Step One

2 pound California Roast, fat trimmed from roast

1 tablespoon extra virgin olive oil

2 strips of bacon

2 tablespoons garlic salt

2 tablespoons black pepper

Step Two

6 large shallots, cut in half and peeled

2 cloves garlic, sliced thick

¼ cup Rabbit Ridge Chardonnay

2 cups water, or enough to cover by 1 inch

1 tablespoon condensed demi-glace or ½ cup beef stock

Step Three

15 tiny boiler onions, ends cut off, blanched in boiling water, drained and peeled under cold water

6 large carrots, peeled and cut into 1 inch pieces

15 small new potatoes

2 tablespoons Pic-a-Peppa sauce

1 cup fresh or frozen peas

Serves 4

Trim fat from roast. Heat olive oil in a large stockpot. Render bacon and fat from roast until browned. Remove bacon and fat from pot and discard. Season roast on all sides with garlic salt and pepper. Brown meat on all sides in rendered fat. Remove meat from pot and set aside.

Add shallots, garlic and wine and deglaze to release brown bit on bottom of pot. Sauté 3 minutes. Place roast back in pot. Add water and demi-glace and simmer 1 hour, partially covered.

Pre-heat oven to 300º. Add onions, carrots, potatoes and Pic-a-Peppa sauce. Simmer 5 minutes. Place pot in oven and finish cooking for 1 more hour. Just before serving, stir in peas and warm.

Recommended Wine
Rabbit Ridge Syrah, Zinfandel, Merlot

First day of harvest: Bins of Estate Chardonnay have just been picked and are ready for crushing.

A forklift is used to dump the bins of Chardonnay grapes into the hopper. The conveyer pulls the grapes through the crusher. Remaining berries are raked into the center.

Chardonnay grapes ready to be dumped in the hopper on the first day of crush at the Paso Robles winery. These Chardonnay grapes were only one of three bins of high quality/low yielding crop.

The grapes travel from the hopper to the de-stemmer, which separates the berries from the stems. The stems are moved on a conveyer belt to a truck that will take them back into the vineyard as organic matter. The crusher breaks the berries open to let the natural yeast get at the juice. White grapes go directly from the crusher to the press. They are then pumped through hoses to tanks in the winery. The juice will ferment there for ten to thirty days.

"The press." (Left)

Stainless tanks ready for white grape juice or red grape "must." (Below)

Pork Tenderloin with Ginger Sauce

This is my version of Pork Robert. It is so delicious, I have to be careful not to sample too much before supper is ready. Pork chops may also be used.

<u>Step One</u>

<u>Serves 8</u>

1 pork tenderloin, trimmed, washed and
   patted dry
1 tablespoon extra virgin olive oil
Salt and pepper to taste

<u>Step Two</u>

½ cup Rabbit Ridge Chardonnay
3 large shallots, minced
3/4 cup veal demi-glace
½ teaspoon soy sauce
1 teaspoon finely minced fresh ginger
1 teaspoon Dijon mustard
1 tablespoon butter
Salt and pepper

<u>Step Three</u>

2 tablespoons fresh parsley, minced

Rub pork all over with extra virgin olive oil, salt and pepper. In a sauté pan on medium-high heat, brown pork on all sides. Remove pork and wrap in foil. Put in a 200° oven for 30 minutes or until internal temperature reaches 160°. Make sure to leave the browned fond (bits and pieces left in the pan) in the bottom of the pan.

Turn heat up to medium. Add wine and shallots to pan. If needed drizzle a tiny bit of extra virgin olive oil in pan to moisten. Sauté shallots 1 minute. Add demi-glace and soy sauce and reduce to half. Add ginger and simmer 2 minutes. Strain into another small pan. Add mustard and simmer on low 1 minute. Just before serving, stir in butter, salt and pepper and all pan drippings.

Slice pork ½ inch. Place slices, over-lapping (fan style), on plates. Drizzle with sauce and top with parsley.

Recommended Wine
Rabbit Ridge Chardonnay, Pinot noir

Our first crop of Pinot noir grapes picked from the Live Oak Vineyard. Only one ton of Pinot noir was crushed from that block of vineyard. This Pinot noir will claim reserve status.

Pork Roast with Lemon and Rosemary

Our housekeeper, Carla, prepared this roast for us while visiting Lecci, a town in the Tuscany region of Italy. Every time I cook this dish, it reminds me of the fabulous food and wine we enjoyed there.

Step One

Serves 4-6

1-3 to 4 lb pork loin roast, split and tied

1 tablespoon extra virgin olive oil

2 tablespoons fresh garlic, finely minced

2 tablespoons lemon zest

2 tablespoons fresh rosemary, finely minced

Salt and pepper to taste

Step Two

1-cup chicken or vegetable stock.

Wash and dry pork. Untie. In a small bowl, combine next 5 ingredients, Divide in half. Spread ½ the mixture inside roast. Re-tie. Rub remaining mixture all over roast. Place on a roasting pan. Let sit until room temperature. Pre-heat oven to 375°. Place stock in a small saucepan. Warm and set aside. Roast pork until internal temperature reaches 160° for medium to 170° for well done. Do not overcook. Remove pork from oven and place on a platter. Let sit 10 minutes. Pour off most of the fat from the roasting pan and place the pan on top of the stove. Turn heat to med-high.

Add stock and scrape the drippings from the pan to combine. Simmer 1 minute, or until slightly thickened. Slice pork. Serve sauce alongside.

Recommended Wine
Rabbit Ridge Chardonnay, Pinot noir, Syrah, Merlot

Roast Prime Rib with Horseradish Sauce

This is a super presentation to serve for guests. I learned of the sauce from my daughter's paternal grandmother. Use regular grated horseradish for the sauce, not cream style. We like a very hot horseradish sauce, but you can decrease the amount of horseradish, if needed. You will need an instant-read thermometer to check doneness.

Step One - Make Sauce

1 - 8 ounce container sour cream

½ cup ground horseradish, drained, pressed completely dry with a spoon.

2 teaspoons dijon mustard

Salt and pepper to taste

Combine all ingredients. Chill.

Step Two

1 prime rib roast, cut off bone and retied (3-4 rib, about 5 lb., bone-in)

2 tablespoon garlic powder

1 tablespoon dry mustard

1 tablespoon coarsely ground salt

1 tablespoon coarsely ground pepper

Combine garlic powder, dry mustard, salt and pepper. Rub generously on top and all sides of roast. Bring meat to room temperature.

Preheat oven to 350°. Place roast in oven, rib side down. Roast until internal temperature registers 130° in the center for rare, (about 1-1½ hours). Adjust cooking time for desired doneness. Remove meat and let sit 25 minutes before carving. Slice and serve with horseradish sauce.

Recommended Wine
Rabbit Ridge Cabernet Sauvignon, Syrah, Zinfandel, Merlot

Veal Chops with Mushroom Demi-Glace

This is a simple and elegant entrée. It is important to use high quality demi-glace.

Step One

Serves 2

½ **cup dried morel mushrooms**
½ **cup Rabbit Ridge Red Wine**

Using a coffee cup, warm wine in microwave for 30 seconds. Place dried morels in wine. Cover and allow mushrooms to reconstitute for 1 hour. Strain and reserve wine for step 3. Use morels in step 2.

Step Two

1 tablespoon unsalted butter
2 veal chops
Salt and pepper to taste
1 shallot, chopped
½ **medium onion, sliced**
1 cup sliced button mushrooms, cleaned
Morel mushrooms from step 1

Melt butter in a medium skillet on medium heat. Season chops with salt and pepper. Add veal chops and brown on both sides. Do not cook through. Remove chops from pan and set aside. Add shallots and onions to pan and sauté 2 minutes. Add morel and button mushrooms and sauté until soft.

Step Three

1 tablespoon fresh thyme leaves
¼ **cup heavy cream**
½ **cup demi-glace**
Reserved wine from step 1
1 teaspoon lemon juice
Pinch of minced lemon rind

Add remaining ingredients to pan. Simmer on low 5 minutes. Place chops back in pan. Turn once to coat with sauce. Cook a few minutes on the stove, or in a warmed oven. Serve with sauce on top or underneath chops.

Recommended Wine
Rabbit Ridge Pinot noir, Sangiovese, Barbera

Veal Osso buco

Veal Osso buco is true comfort food to me. I always serve this when I have company that enjoys home cooking. Browning the veal shanks well is a must. Try not to disturb the shanks until they are completely browned.

Step One

2 tablespoons unsalted butter
2 tablespoons extra virgin olive oil
½ cup flour
Salt and pepper
6-8 veal shanks, washed and dried

Step Two

1 ½ cup onions, peeled
1 cup carrots, peeled
¾ cup celery, washed
2 cloves garlic
½ cup Rabbit Ridge Chardonnay
1 cup veal demi-glace
2 tablespoons tomato paste
¼ teaspoon ground cinnamon
¼ teaspoon ground cumin
½ teaspoon fresh thyme leaves
1 teaspoon fresh basil leaves
2 bay leaves

Serves 6

Place butter and olive oil in a large Dutch oven and place on the stove. Season veal with salt and pepper. Lightly flour veal chops on both sides. Heat butter and oil until shimmering. Place as many shanks in the pan that will fit in a single layer. Brown well on both sides. Repeat with remaining shanks until all are well browned on both sides. Remove shanks to a plate and keep warm. Remove pan from heat. Pre-heat oven to 350º.

Chop onions, carrots, celery, and garlic in a processor. Place pan back on stove, and turn up to med-high heat. Add vegetables. Sauté 2 minutes. Add wine and deglaze, scraping all the brown bits from the bottom of the pan. Add veal demi-glace and tomato paste and stir to combine. Cook 2 minutes. Add remaining spices and herbs, and stir. Place veal back in pan and turn to coat. Spoon some of the sauce over the top of the meat. Cover and bake in the oven 1-½ hours, until meat is tender. Periodically spoon sauce over veal. Add more wine if sauce becomes too dry. Plate veal and pour sauce on top.

Garnish with fresh minced parsley, basil or chopped roasted garlic, if desired.

Recommended Wine
Rabbit Ridge Syrah, Zinfandel, Primitivo, Petite Sirah

While we were visiting Castallina in Chianti, my family and I found this great meat store. The rock walls were covered with hanging salami, prosciutto, sausages and Cinghiale (boar). A large mortadella salami sat ready to be sliced for customers.

New American Oak Demptos barrels waiting to be filled.

WINERY ACTIVITIES and POULTRY

Chicken marinated in Hoisin Sauce

Marinades are great because you can prepare them in the morning. When it is time for supper, just light the grill. This marinade is wonderful, so baste the chicken often while cooking.

Step One

Serves 4

2 large scallions
  or 4 small scallions
3 cloves fresh garlic
1 –1/2 inch x 1/2 inch piece of fresh ginger, peeled
2 teaspoons sliced lemon grass

Place scallions, garlic, ginger and lemon grass in a mini processor. Finely chop. Scrape into a mixing bowl or a small container.

Step Two

2 tablespoon extra virgin olive oil
2 tablespoons worchester
2 teaspoons hoisin sauce

Stir extra virgin olive oil, white worchester, and hoisin sauce into mixture from step 1. Set aside.

Step Three

4 single chicken breasts, with skin and bone, or without
Salt and white pepper to taste
Rice (optional)

Wash and dry chicken breasts. Pat dry. Remove any remaining fat. Place chicken in a glass container and coat with marinade. Refrigerate at least 2 hours. Just before cooking, brush off excess marinade. Season with salt and pepper. Grill, bake or sauté until just cooked through. Baste if needed. Serve with rice.

Recommended Wine
Rabbit Ridge Viognier, Syrah, Primitivo, Zinfandel

Red wine during a "pump-over."

Hopper to Tank: *Every month is hectic when operating a winery and caring for numerous vineyards. Although harvest is the most intense time of the year, every month plays a major part in the process of growing high quality wine grapes and producing world-class wines.*

After the red grapes are crushed, they are pumped into tanks to ferment. Red grapes usually ferment for four to twelve days. This is shorter than white grapes because the tannic skins of red grapes are left in the tank with the juice, therefore providing more nutrients to activate the yeast. After fermentation, the red grape juice has become wine. The wine continues to sit in the tanks for twelve to thirty days for extended maceration (skin contact), which draws out the color and gives character to the wine. During this time, numerous pump-overs are done to the red juice to ensure that all of the liquid comes into contact with the skins.

Once the red juice finishes maceration, it is sent back to the press. After pressing, the juice is pumped into stainless steel tanks to settle before going to barrels.

After the wine is pressed, it is moved to barrels.

Fermentation*: In order for the grape juice to ferment, additions need to be made. Even though SO_2 is a natural product of fermentation, sulfur dioxide additions are a normal part of winemaking. SO_2 is added for the same reason lemon juice is brushed on an open apple. SO_2 prevents discoloration from oxygen. In addition, it also kills wild yeast and unwanted bacteria. Winery laws require a statement on the label that wine contains sulfites.*

Wine is usually fermented by inoculating it with yeast. Fermentation can also be naturally occurring. Wine can ferment in wooden tanks, concrete tanks, plastic boxes, stainless steel tanks (usually with a closed top, but can be left open-topped) Rabbit Ridge uses French and American oak barrels and stainless tanks.

As wine ferments, heat is produced. The heat is caused by glucose turning to alcohol plus carbon dioxide. Since yeast will not grow with temperatures over 100 degrees or under 50 degrees, wine tanks are usually temperature controlled.

Pressing: *Pressing is done to squeeze the liquid out of the solids. Blush and white wines are pressed before fermentation; red wines are pressed after fermentation. There are a few types of pressings. "Free-run" is done without crushing the grapes and therefore produces the highest quality wine with less tannins, bitterness and astringency. "Press fractions" and "hard press" are two other pressing methods. A winemaker must know what type of press and related equipment will be needed to produce a specific result.*

Typically a winemaker can expect 140-190 gallons of juice per one ton of grapes. The skins and seeds left after pressing are called "pomace." Red grape pomace is hand-shoveled out of the press after all the juice is removed. It is spread back into the vineyard as organic matter.

Barrels filled with fermenting chardonnay bubble into containers filled with water. The bubble are caused by CO_2 being released during fermentation.

Barrels stacked for aging - up to 30 months

Topping **& Aging:** *After fermentation takes place, the wine is moved to barrels to age. Many time-consuming procedures have to be done regularly to the wine at this stage to maintain the quality and integrity of the wine. Once the wine is in the barrels, "topping" a barrel of wine is done to fill the space that is created from evaporation which occurs over time. Since oxygen is detrimental to wine, the barrels are topped with more wine to fill the barrel to the top. Moving barrels of wine into place for topping takes long hours of fork lift work. It takes two people over 1 month to top our barrels.*

After the wine has aged an appropriate amount of time, it is pumped back to the tank to be blended or held. After blending, the wine is ready to be filtered.

Chicken Piccata with Rosemary

Chicken breasts sautéed with lemon and butter are delightful. I have added rosemary to enhance and deepen the sauce. If you do not like rosemary, use fresh basil. Veal scallopini may also be used.

Step One

2 chicken breasts, skinned, boned
   and trimmed of any fat

Step Two

½ cup flour

½ - 1 teaspoon salt and pepper to taste

2 tablespoons extra virgin olive oil

2 tablespoons butter

Step Three

1-2 tablespoons lemon juice

¼ cup Rabbit Ridge Chardonnay

½ cup chicken stock

2 sprigs fresh rosemary

1 tablespoon butter

Step Four

1 tablespoon capers, drained and rinsed

1 tablespoon fresh parsley, minced

Rice (optional)

2 lemons, seeds removed and sliced thin

Serves 2

Preheat oven to 200°. Wash and dry chicken. Place chicken between two pieces of wax paper and pound thin. Set aside.

Place flour, salt and pepper in a zip-lock baggie. Place chicken in seasoned flour mixture and shake. Remove chicken from baggie and shake off excess flour. Heat oil and butter in a frying pan until shimmering. Sauté chicken on both sides until brown but not cooked through. Remove chicken from pan and place on a plate in the warmed oven.

Add lemon, wine, chicken stock, rosemary, and butter to the frying pan. Simmer on Med-low heat until thickened.

Return chicken to pan and turn to coat. Place capers and parsley on top. Cover and simmer 2 minutes. Remove rosemary sprigs. Plate chicken and serve with rice, if desired. Pour all pan drippings on top of chicken. Garnish with lemon slices and fresh rosemary sprigs. Serve hot.

Recommended Wine

Rabbit Ridge Chardonnay or Sauvignon Blanc

Grilled Chicken with Sage

My sister Sandy loves marinades, especially ones that use a lot of garlic. Experimenting with different herbs is fun to do here. This chicken would be great sliced and served cold in a salad.

Step One

¼ cup extra virgin olive oil

1 - 2 cloves fresh garlic, chopped

Zest of 1 lemon

1 tablespoon fresh sage, minced

Salt and pepper to taste

2 tablespoons red onions, minced

Step Two

2 whole chicken breasts, or 4 single breasts, skinned, boned, and trimmed of any fat

Serves 4

Mix all ingredients.

Wash and dry chicken. Place chicken between two pieces of wax paper and pound to ¼ inch thick. Be careful not to rip the breast meat. Place chicken in marinade from step 1 and refrigerate all day, or at least 2 hours. Grill chicken, basting often for 2 to 3 minutes per side.

Optional serving suggestion- after grilling, place one fresh sage leaf on top of chicken breast, cover sage with a thin slice of Parma Prosciutto. Top prosciutto with shaved Fontina Cheese. Broil 5 minutes, or until lightly browned.

Recommended Wine
Rabbit Ridge Chardonnay or Sauvignon Blanc

Filtering: *While the wine is in stainless steel tanks, "settling" occurs and either racking or filtering is done to separate the juice from the solids. The solid sediment left in the barrels is called "lees" which is simply the residual grape and yeast solids.*

Some wines are filtered and fined. Others are not. The grape varietal and how well the wine behaves while aging can determine how much sediment needs to be removed. Filtering is done by inserting special wine pads into a rack. The wine is pumped through the filter pads and then back into a clean tank. If the wine is very dense with sediment, filtering can take all night. After filtering, the wine is ready to bottle.

Roast Turkey

Turkey is so healthy, especially when eaten without the skin. This procedure will give you a very nicely flavored skin for those of you who prefer to eat it.

Step One

Serves 4-6

1 whole fresh turkey
Cooking string (usually comes with turkey)

Step Two

1 whole head of fresh garlic, outer skin
   removed, cloves left intact
1 whole medium onion, unpeeled
Salt and pepper for cavity of turkey
1 tablespoon extra virgin olive oil
2 tablespoons garlic salt
Freshly ground Pepper to taste
16 ounces low-salt chicken stock

Pre-heat oven to 375º, or recommended temperature from turkey instructions. Remove bags from inside of turkey. There can be two, one in front and one in back of the cavity. Rinse inside and outside of turkey and dry completely. Place turkey in a large roasting pan with sides at least 2 inches high. Place cooking string under ends of turkey to help lift when ready to remove from oven.

Cut off top of garlic head. Cut unpeeled onion in half. Insert garlic and onion into cavity of turkey. Season cavity generously with salt and pepper. Rub turkey with olive oil, sprinkle with garlic salt and pepper. Place turkey in oven and pour chicken stock into pan. Cook turkey until juices run clear from thigh when pierced with a toothpick, or recommended cooking time from turkey directions based on weight.

Remove turkey from oven and place on a platter. Strain drippings into a small saucepan. Add more stock to make 2 cups. Keep warm. Serve immediately or thicken with a little flour for gravy.

To make gravy, dissolve 1-tablespoon flour into 1-tablespoon cold chicken stock, add to warm stock and boil until thickened. Repeat flour procedure until desired consistency is achieved. Carve turkey and serve with stock or gravy.

Recommended Wine
Rabbit Ridge Chardonnay or Pinot noir

Todd's Lemon Chicken

I created this chicken marinade for our good friend Todd Williams of Toad Hollow Winery. Todd and his wife, Frankie, wanted a grilled chicken recipe that did not contain any salt. This is great served as a kabob.

Step One

2 tablespoons honey
½ cup red wine vinegar
1 cup extra virgin olive oil
4 onions, chopped
3 tablespoons "Herb, Garlic, No Salt Spices"
Zest of 1 lemon
1/4 cup lemon juice
1 tablespoon fresh thyme
1 tablespoon dried tarragon
Black pepper to taste

Step Two

4 whole chicken breast, boneless and skinless; washed and patted dry

Serves 8

Combine all ingredients.

Slice or cube chicken. Place on skewers. Pour marinade over chicken. Marinate overnight, or at least 4 hours, turning often. Grill or sauté.

Recommended Wine
Rabbit Ridge Sauvignon Blanc

Turkey Sausage

I created this recipe because I love sausage, but do not like the fat. Soy sauce enhances the color and flavor of the turkey.

Step One

Serves 4-6

1 tablespoon extra virgin olive oil
½ cup shallots, minced
2 cloves garlic, minced
¼ cup parsley, minced

Sauté shallots, garlic and parsley in extra virgin olive oil until soft, about 5 minutes.

Step Two

1 pound ground turkey
½ teaspoon ground sage
½ teaspoon fennel seed, finely crushed
½ teaspoon garlic powder
¼ teaspoon crushed red pepper
1 tablespoon fresh cilantro, minced
4 tablespoons soy sauce
Salt and pepper to taste

Place turkey in a large bowl. Add shallot mixture from step 1. Add remaining ingredients and mix well. Shape into patties. Fry in a sauté pan sprayed with Pam until well browned. If needed, wrap in foil and finish cooking in the oven at 350º for 5-10 minutes.

Recommended Wine
Rabbit Ridge Pinot noir, Syrah

FALL'S REST AND SEAFOOD ENTRÉES

Ahi Tuna with Soy and Wasabi

I created this dish for our first open house party in Paso Robles, California. The neighbors loved it. We prefer ahi tuna, but any fresh tuna will work.

Step One

2 Fresh Ahi, Yellow Fin, or Albacore tuna steaks
1 tablespoon soy sauce
Freshly ground pepper

Step Two

4 tablespoon soy sauce
½ teaspoon sesame oil
1-2 teaspoons fresh garlic, minced
1-2 teaspoons fresh ginger, minced
1 teaspoon dijon mustard
½ teaspoon wasabi paste
1 teaspoon dry sherry

Serves 2

Place tuna in a glass container and coat with soy. Let marinate 30 minutes, but no longer. Remove from soy and pat dry. Season both sides with pepper.

Combine all ingredients. Set aside to serve with Ahi.

Preparation: Heat a non-stick pan, lightly coated with olive oil. Quickly sear both sides of tuna on medium-high heat, about 1 minute each. Remove from heat. Slice thin and serve with extra sauce on the side. Adjust cooking time for medium temperature. Garnish with thinly sliced scallions

Recommended Wine
Rabbit Ridge Viognier, Sparkling Wine, Chardonnay

The first show of fall on the Chardonnay vines.

Fall is one of the prettiest times in the vineyard because the leaves from the grape varietals turn different colors. For example, Chardonnay turns gold, Pinot noir changes to a pale magenta, Syrah transforms to a ruby red while Cabernet becomes purple.

Grilled Lobster

This is a delicious lobster presentation. The only chore is cutting the lobsters in half.

<u>**Step One**</u>   <u>*Serves 2-4*</u>

2 whole lobster tails

<u>**Step Two**</u>

2 tablespoons extra-virgin olive oil
2 tablespoons unsalted butter, melted
Salt and pepper to taste

Cut each lobster tail completely in half down the center. Pull lobster meat out of the shell, in one piece. Rinse with cold water and place back in its shell.

Pre-heat grill to high. Place the tails, shell side down, on the grill. Drizzle each tail with extra virgin olive oil and butter. Season with salt and pepper. Grill until the lobsters begin to sizzle around the edges of the shell and the meat begins to turn white. Lower heat to low and continue to cook until lobster meat is white. Do not over cook the lobsters.

Assembly: Remove lobster meat from its shell. Serve the lobsters whole or sliced into medallions, with lemon wedges, butter or a complimentary sauce.

Recommended Wine
Rabbit Ridge Chardonnay

Grilled Salmon with Dijon

When I simply do not have the time or energy, I prepare this salmon dish. It is quick, uses very few ingredients, and it is full of flavor.

Step One

4 fresh salmon filets
2 tablespoons dijon
1 tablespoon Rabbit Ridge Chardonnay
1 tablespoon extra virgin olive oil
Salt and pepper

Serves 4

Wash and dry fish. Season with salt and pepper. Combine dijon, wine and extra virgin olive oil. Brush generously on salmon. Grill or bake until meat is juicy and flakes with a fork. Do not overcook

Cooking Note: If you buy your salmon filet with the skin on one side, do not worry. Follow all steps and grill or bake with the skin side down until cooked or very charred. Turn fish to dijon side and peel off skin with a spoon. Scrape all brown off. When topside is brown, turn back to the scraped side to insure fish is cooked. Be careful not to tear the fish while turning.

Recommended Wine
Rabbit Ridge Chardonnay, Pinot noir

Fall colors in the Live Oak Vineyard.

Grilled Shrimp and Scallops with Corn Salsa

These skewers have a wonderful smoky flavor from the grill. I prefer using good quality metal skewers because they are very sturdy and will not burn. However, wooden skewers will work as long as they are soaked in water at least one hour before grilling.

Step One

Serves 2-4

3 ears of fresh corn, cooked

1 red pepper, small dice

Juice of ½ lime

2 teaspoons fresh ginger, minced

Pinch of sugar

1 teaspoon pear vinegar

1 teaspoon extra virgin olive oil

1 tablespoon fresh basil, minced

Salt and pepper to taste

Step Two

1 tablespoon extra virgin olive oil

2 cloves garlic, minced

Pinch of curry

Pinch of cumin

1 tablespoon dried basil

Salt and pepper to taste

Step Three

1 pound fresh jumbo shrimp

½ pound fresh scallops

Cut corn off cobs. Place in a plastic bowl. Add remaining step one ingredients and toss. Cover and chill until ready to serve.

Sauté garlic, cumin and curry in extra virgin olive oil for 1 minute. Do not burn. Add basil, salt and pepper. Remove from heat.

Peel and devein shrimp. Wash scallops. Pat seafood dry. Place in marinade from step two. Chill in the refrigerator at least 1 hour, turning frequently. Put shrimp and scallops on skewers. Grill about 2 minutes on each side on a high flame or until lightly charred.

Assembly: Use a slotted spoon to drain liquid from corn, place salsa on serving plates. Remove shrimp and scallops from skewers, or serve on skewer. Place seafood on top of salsa, alternating shrimp and scallops in a circular pattern.

Recommended Wine
Rabbit Ridge Sauvignon blanc, Viognier

Grilled Swordfish with Mango Salsa

This is the most fabulous tasting dish with very little fat. Please purchase only fresh swordfish. The best way to tell is to make sure that the dark part in the steak is bright red or pink. Every time I make this dish, I think of my great friend, Marijane, who lives in Fort Lauderdale, Florida. Marijane has dozens of Mango trees growing in her yard.

Step One - Prepare Mango

1 ripe mango, peeled
Note: I peel mangos with a very sharp vegetable peeler.

Step Two: Prepare Salsa

½ red bell pepper, seeded
½ yellow bell pepper, seeded
½ cucumber, peeled, cut in half length-
   wise, seeds scooped out with a spoon
1 teaspoon lime juice
¼ cup red onion, finely chopped
2 tablespoons fresh cilantro, minced
1 fresh jalapeño, seeded, finely minced
½ teaspoon fresh ginger, minced
Pinch of sugar

Step Three

4 fresh swordfish steaks
Salt and pepper to taste

Serves 4

Hold the peeled mango, upright, like a football just before a punt. Using a sharp knife, slice down the side to remove the meat. Do not cut too close to the seed or the fruit will become grainy. Slice into even strips, and then dice. Place in a bowl.

Slice the peppers and cucumber into small, even-sized strips, then finely dice. Add to the bowl with the mangos. Add remaining ingredients and stir. Chill. Use only as much jalapeño as desired.

Rinse and dry swordfish. Season both sides with salt and pepper. Grill on medium-high heat. Do not overcook. Swordfish is much better just barely cooked. Place swordfish on plates. Top with mango salsa.

Recommended Wine
Rabbit Ridge Sauvignon blanc, Viognier

Grilled Swordfish with Tomato Basil Sauce

I created this sauce when my basil in Florida grew to four feet high. I could not find enough uses for it. Pesto was the answer. Although the traditional pesto never appealed to me, the simple combination of garlic and basil mixed with tomato is great.

Step One - Make Sauce

Serves 4

2 strips of bacon

3 tablespoons extra virgin olive oil

6 plum tomatoes, seeded and sliced

1 shallot, minced

1 clove garlic, minced

¼ cup fresh basil, minced

Salt and pepper to taste

1 teaspoon balsamic vinegar, optional

Place bacon in a large frying pan and cook until all the fat is rendered. Remove bacon from pan and place on a paper towel. Add oil and shallot to fat and sauté. Break bacon into tiny pieces and add back to pan with remaining ingredients. Simmer until tomatoes are soft. Add balsamic vinegar, if desired.

Step Two

4 fresh swordfish steaks

Salt and pepper to taste

Rinse and dry swordfish. Season both sides with salt and pepper. Grill on medium-high heat. Do not overcook. Serve with sauce on top.

Recommended Wine

Rabbit Ridge Chardonnay, Merlot

Grouper with Capers, Lemon and Herbes de Provence

This is my version of Grouper Meunière.' The traditional French version of Dover Sole Meunière is bathed in butter. Unfortunately, once you have had the buttery version, it is hard to have anything but the real thing. For nights when I need to keep the calories down, I opt for my lower fat counterpart. Any light, white fish may be substituted for the grouper.

Step One

1 tablespoons extra virgin olive oil

1 tablespoon butter

1 teaspoon ground Herbes de Provence

Step Two

4 grouper filets, cleaned, washed and dried (½ lb. per person)

Salt and pepper to taste

1/8 teaspoon garlic powder

Step Three

1 tablespoon capers, rinsed

Juice of ½ lemon,

Lemon slices from ½ lemon

1 tablespoon fresh parsley, chopped

Serves 4

Place extra virgin olive oil, butter and Herbes de Provence in a cool sauté pan. Stir to combine.

Season fish with salt, pepper and garlic powder. Heat pan from step one to medium-high heat. Sauté fish until brown, about 3 minutes. Turn. Cook on other side.

Swirl in capers and lemon juice. Simmer until fish is cooked through and nicely brown. Allow lemon juice to reduce to a syrup. Sprinkle with parsley and serve with lemon slices. Do not overcook. If needed, finish cooking in the over at 350º .

Recommended Wine
Rabbit Ridge Sauvignon blanc, Chardonnay

Herbed Garlic Mussels

Mussels are so delicious served in a large bowl with bread on the side for dipping. These mussels could also be served over pasta.

Step One

Serves 2-4

2 pounds mussels

Step Two

2 tablespoons butter
2 tablespoons extra virgin olive oil
3 cloves fresh garlic, roughly chopped
½ cup chopped onion
½ cup Rabbit Ridge Chardonnay
2 tomatoes, seeded and chopped
1 teaspoon fresh basil, chopped
½ teaspoon fresh thyme, minced
Pinch of salt to taste
½ cup reserved mussel liquid

Scrub and clean mussels. Soak mussels in water for 1 hour. Remove mussels with tongs. Set aside for step 2. Strain liquid in a paper towel lined colander. Reserve ½ cup liquid. Discard any open mussels.

In a medium pot, sauté garlic and onions in butter and olive oil for 2 minutes. Do not burn. Add remaining ingredients and bring to a boil. Lower heat and simmer for 1 minute. Place mussels from step one in pot and steam until shells open, about 10 minutes.

Assembly: Remove mussels from pot. Discard any mussels that did not open. Break off one side of the shell that holds the mussel. Discard the unused other shell. Arrange mussels in their shells on a platter or bowl and keep warm. Strain cooking liquid again, place back in a smaller pan and simmer until reduced by ½. Pour sauce over mussels and serve warm.

Recommended Wine
Rabbit Ridge Chardonnay, Sauvignon Blanc

Raw Oysters with Shallot Vinaigrette

I first enjoyed a flavorful vinaigrette served with raw oysters at a restaurant in Sonoma County called John Ash, and Co. Recently, I enjoyed something similar at Le Cirque in New York. It is still my favorite accompaniment to serve with raw oysters.

Step One

1 cup white wine vinegar

¼ cup fresh lemon juice

2 large shallots, minced

Salt to taste

1 tablespoon freshly ground pepper

Step Two

4 dozen fresh raw oysters

Serves 4

Combine all ingredients. Set aside.

Have your fishmonger shuck the oysters just before needed. Or, if you are proficient at shucking, like my brother-in-law, Stephen McKeithen, you can do it yourself. Place on seaweed, rock salt or a towel lined platter. Serve with vinaigrette.

Oysters and stonecrabs in Florida.

Recommended Wine
Rabbit Ridge Sauvignon blanc, Champagne, Chardonnay

Four weeks after harvest and leaf change, the vines drop all foliage and the second crop that did not make the cut for harvest. Like a salmon at the end of its river run, the vines are worn out from months of growth and fruit bearing. It is time for the vines to rest and rebuild energy.

Salmon en Pappillot with Leeks, Carrots and Wine

This is a rather healthy salmon preparation. The reduced stock and wine cooked over the fish create a lovely sauce.

Step One   *Serves 2*

2 salmon fillets, all skin removed   Wash and dry fish. Season with salt and
Salt and pepper to taste   pepper. Refrigerate until ready to cook.

Step Two

1 cup chicken stock   Boil chicken stock until reduced by ½.
¼ cup Rabbit Ridge Chardonnay   Add wine and pepper. Reduce again for
Pinch of white pepper   2 minutes.

Step Three

1 leek, white part only, julienne cut   Heat extra virgin olive oil in a sauté pan
1 celery stalk, julienne cut   until shimmering. Add vegetables and sauté
2 carrots, julienne cut   until tender but not cooked through. Add
1 tablespoon fresh parsley, minced   parsley and toss.
3 tablespoons extra virgin olive oil
1 tablespoon unsalted butter   **Assembly:** Place salmon on a lightly oiled
                                                                        piece of foil or parchment. Place vegetables
Note: julienne cut are very thin   on top of the salmon, drizzle sauce on top,
matchstick slices.   and seal. Bake at 350º until fish is tender
                                                                        but not dry, about 15- 25 minutes. Top with
                                                                        additional butter if desired.

Recommended Wine
Rabbit Ridge Chardonnay, Pinot noir

PRUNING SEASON and SALADS

Belgian Endive with Warm Goat Cheese and Grainy Mustard

Soft, warm goat cheese tastes incredible with chilled endive. The grainy mustard adds the perfect tang.

Serves 2

Step One - Make Vinaigrette

½ cup extra virgin olive oil
¼ cup white wine vinegar
2 tablespoons grainy mustard
1 teaspoon lemon juice
1 teaspoon white worchester sauce
Pinch sugar, pinch salt, pinch pepper

Whisk all ingredients. Store in refrigerator for up to five days.

Step Two

1 small head bibb lettuce, washed and dried
4 heads Belgian endive leaves separated,
   washed and dried

Tear bibb into bite-sized pieces. Place on salad plates. Place endive on one side of the salad plate; cut side toward the center, in a fan shape.

Step Three

1 package goat cheese

Slice goat cheese with a wet knife into ¼ inch rounds. Place on a piece of aluminum foil. Bake 2 minutes at 250º.

Assembly: Slide warmed goat cheese onto opposite side of salad plate from endive. Push leaves toward the center of the plate so that they touch the cheese. Drizzle with mustard vinaigrette.

Recommended Wine
Rabbit Ridge Sauvignon blanc, Chardonnay

Chicken Salad with Tarragon

Today, many grocery stores roast fresh chickens in their deli. Do not use flavored chickens such as: barbecue flavor. However, lemon-pepper seasoning works great.

Step One

1 whole roasted chicken, about 2 cups meat

Step Two

½ cup Hellmann's or Best Foods mayonnaise
2 stalks celery, finely diced
2 teaspoons fresh tarragon, finely chopped
2 scallions, finely chopped
Salt and pepper to taste

Serves 2-4

Remove all meat from chicken and discard skin. Use bones to make chicken stock or discard. Cut chicken into bite-size pieces.

Combine chicken with mayonnaise, celery, tarragon, scallions, salt and pepper. Do not stir too hard or you will tear the chicken pieces. Serve on lettuce or on bread as a sandwich.

Recommended Wine
Rabbit Ridge Chardonnay

Erich's Tomato Salad

When I first started dating Erich, he used to make this salad for lunch. The garden at Rabbit Ridge provides us with a bounty of fresh tomatoes to enjoy all summer. There is nothing like picking fresh tomatoes and eating them that day.

Step One

2 large tomatoes, seeded

Step Two

2 tablespoons extra virgin olive oil
1 tablespoon balsamic vinegar
Pinch dried sweet basil
Salt and pepper to taste

Serves 2

Slice tomatoes. Place in a salad bowl.

Whisk together dressing and pour on tomatoes and toss. Drain if necessary before serving.

Recommended Wine
Rabbit Ridge Zinfandel

Pruning: *The previous years pruning will affect the next years crop. Each vine is pruned one bud up from the base of the cordon. Some wineries and vineyards prune two or three buds up to increase the crop to make more money. However "over-cropping" will lessen the quality of the fruit. Rabbit Ridge prefers lower yielding vines for better wine quality.*

Fresh Mushroom and Arugula Salad

Erich and I had a salad like this in Florence, Italy, while dining with my sister Kathy and brother-in-law Stephen. The original salad used sliced raw artichoke hearts as well as mushrooms. I have omitted the artichoke hearts because I have not been able to find the sweet baby type with comparable flavor as those used in Italy.

Step One

1 pound fresh button mushroom

Step Two

3 cups fresh arugula, washed and dried
½ cup Parmigiano-Reggiano, shaved

Step Three

Vinaigrette from page 150
Salt and pepper to taste

Serves 2-4

Wipe mushrooms clean with a damp paper towel. Trim stems and slice ¼ inch thick.

Plate arugula. Top with sliced mushrooms and shaved Parmigiano-Reggiano.

Whisk together dressing and serve with salad. Season with salt and pepper to taste.

Recommended Wine
Rabbit Ridge Sauvignon Blanc, Pinot noir

Fruit Ambrosia

My mother's Aunt Sara used to make this delightful fruit salad for beach parties on Miami Beach in the 40's. It is very simple and refreshing.

Step One

Serves 4

1 cup low fat sour cream

1 can pineapple chunks, drained

1 can mandarin oranges, drained

1 cup miniature marshmallows

1 cup flaked coconut

1 tablespoon cointreau

Combine all ingredients. Cover and refrigerate for several hours.

Recommended Wine
Rabbit Ridge White Zinfandel, Viognier

Green Salad with Arugula and Red Pepper

Erich and I love arugula. This salad could also be made without lettuce, using only arugula and peppers.

Step One - Make Vinaigrette

Serves 2-4

½ cup extra virgin olive oil

¼ cup red wine vinegar

1 teaspoon dijon mustard

1 teaspoon lemon juice

1 teaspoon white worchester sauce

Pinch sugar

Pinch salt

Pinch pepper

Whisk all ingredients. Store in refrigerator for up to five days.

Step Two:

1 bunch mild lettuce

1 bunch arugula, stemmed

1 red bell pepper, cut in julienne

Clean greens and tear into pieces. Wrap in a moist paper towel. Put in a plastic baggie and refrigerate until ready to serve. Plate lettuce and arugula and top with red pepper. Serve with dressing.

Recommended Wine
Rabbit Ridge Sauvignon blanc

Green Salad with Asiago and Olives

We eat salads as our main course on many days. This salad has just about everything in it you need for a satisfying meal.

Step One   *Serves 2-4*

1 egg

Simmer egg on medium-low for 30 minutes. Remove from heat and run under cold water for a few minutes. Peel and chop.

Step Two

1 head or 1 bag of salad greens of choice

Clean greens and tear into pieces. Wrap in a moist paper towel. Put in a plastic baggie and refrigerate until ready to serve.

Step Three

1 large red bell pepper, diced small
1 large tomato, seeded and diced small
1 cup frozen peas, thawed
¼ cup red onion, minced
½ cup carrot, shredded or small dice
3 stalks celery, small dice
5 large green olives, minced

Place lettuce, chopped egg and vegetables in a large salad bowl.

Step Four

1 cup shredded Asiago cheese

Toss salad with cheese and dressing of choice. Note: any cheese can be used.

Salad dressing of choice

I like to mix 2 parts of my vinaigrette and 1 part prepared ranch dressing. Then I add 1 tablespoon white or dark balsamic vinegar.

Recommended Wine
Rabbit Ridge Sauvignon blanc, Chardonnay

Green Salad with Watercress and Tomatoes

This is another simple salad. The flavor of watercress is so refreshing. Be sure to remove any tough stems on the watercress before washing.

<hr>

Step One Make Vinaigrette

Serves 2

½ cup extra virgin olive oil

¼ cup red or white wine vinegar

1 teaspoon dijon mustard

1 teaspoon lemon juice

1 teaspoon white worchester

Pinch of sugar

Pinch of salt

Pinch of pepper

Whisk all ingredients. Store in refrigerator for up to five days.

Step Two

1 head bibb lettuce, washed and dried

1 bunch watercress, washed, stemmed, and dried

2 tomatoes, washed, seeded and diced

Plate greens. Top with chopped tomatoes and vinaigrette.

Recommended Wine
Rabbit Ridge Chardonnay, Sauvignon blanc

Jocelyn's Caesar Salad

This is one of my best friend's recipes. Jocelyn Fagan is remarkable. She is a physical therapist, a mother of three girls and she cooks almost every night for her family. She has substituted the traditional egg yolk with mayonnaise, which I think creates a lighter style ceasar dressing.

Step One   Serves 4

1 head romaine lettuce

Wash and dry lettuce. Tear into large pieces. Place in a large salad bowl.

Step Two

4 tablespoon extra virgin olive oil
1 tablespoons red wine vinegar
1 clove garlic, pressed and minced
2 tablespoon Hellmann's Mayonnaise
Juice of ½ lemon
1 teaspoon worcestershire
2 anchovies, rinsed, dried and pureed
½ cup Parmigiano-Reggiano, grated
Lots of fresh ground black pepper
Salt to taste
Croutons - fresh or ready-made

Process or puree first 7 ingredients. Toss with salad greens. Add Parmigiano-Reggiano, salt and pepper and toss. Serve immediately with croutons.

Recommended Wine
Rabbit Ridge Chardonnay, Sauvignon blanc

Sunrise in Paso Robles

Mom's Southern Cole Slaw

My mother makes this cole slaw for many of our family gatherings. It is the freshest and best tasting cole slaw I have tasted. The original recipe may have come from an old southern cookbook, but my mother is not sure where it originated.

Step One

Serves 4

1 cup Hellmanns or Best Foods mayonnaise
2 teaspoon sugar
½ teaspoon salt
1 teaspoon cider vinegar
1 teaspoon celery seed

Mix all ingredients.

Step Two

3 cups shredded cabbage
1 large tomato, seeded and diced

Add cabbage to mayonnaise and stir. Add tomatoes and toss.

Recommended Wine
Rabbit Ridge Chardonnay

Masterful pruning is part of perfectly farmed grape vines. Pruning the vine is as important as crushing the fruit. It must be done right.

Tomato, Basil, Mozzarella Salad

Make sure to invest in good quality fresh buffalo or cow's milk mozzarella. There is no substitution. To cut basil, place leaves on top of each other, roll like a cigar, and thinly slice.

<u>**Step One:**</u> **Vinaigrette**

<u>*Serves 2*</u>

½ **cup extra virgin olive oil**

1/8 - ¼ **cup white wine vinegar**

1 teaspoon Dijon mustard

1 teaspoon balsamic vinegar

Pinch of sugar

Salt and pepper to taste

Wisk all vinaigrette ingredients.

<u>**Step Two**</u>

3 ripe plum, beefsteak, or vine ripened
  tomatoes, and sliced

1 large ball of fresh buffalo or cow's milk
  mozzarella, rinsed, drained and sliced
  ¼ **inch**

6 large fresh basil leaves, cut into thin
  strips (Chiffonade)

Alternate fresh tomato slices and mozzarella slices in a single row on a plate. Evenly distribute basil leaves over mozzarella and tomato.

Assembly: Salad can be prepared uniformly as stated above, or tossed loosely together.

Recommended Wine
Rabbit Ridge Zinfandel, Primitivo

BOTTLING and LABELING and DESSERTS

Apple Crisp

Erich doesn't like pies. (He worked in a pie factory when he was young). I make this dessert instead of apple pie.

Step One

Serves 2

2 granny smith apples
1 teaspoon fresh lemon juice

Peel and slice apples. Sprinkle with lemon juice. Set aside.

Step Two

3 tablespoons unsalted butter
2 tablespoons brown sugar
½ teaspoon ground cinnamon
1 teaspoon lemon rind, grated
1 teaspoon flour
2 teaspoons Captain Morgan spiced rum

Melt butter in a saucepan. Add brown sugar, cinnamon, and lemon rind. Cook 1 minute. Add apples and cook 1 more minute, stirring to combine. Sprinkle flour over apples, add rum and stir. Cook 1 additional minute.

Step Three

½ cup shortbread cookies

Place cookies in a processor and finely crush. Grease a small casserole or low-sided gratin dish with butter. Pour apples into dish and top with ground cookies. Bake at 350° for 5 minutes. Make sure not to burn the cookies. Serve over ice cream or alone.

Bottling: *When it is time to bottle, the wine flows by gravity from the tank to the bottling machine. The machine disperses the right amount of wine into each bottle, inserts the cork, places the capsule and applies the label on the bottle. Experienced management is needed to oversee the numerous steps that occur simultaneously.*

It takes five to eight people to run the Rabbit Ridge bottling machine. This is a million dollar machine and worth respecting. Prior to filling the bottles with wine, the machine and bottles are sterilized. It can take hours to days to complete a specific bottling. Many times we work straight through the night to finish the work.

Fresh Berries with Zabaglione

This is our favorite dessert. I found this version from an Epicurious letter from Piedmont; master chef, Cesare Giaccone, of Da Cesare restaurant in Albaretto Della Torre, Italy. Most Zabaglione is made with Marsala, but I like this version, which uses Moscato d'Asti. Spinetta Moscato d'Asti is our favorite brand.

Step One

1 cup fresh raspberries
1 cup fresh blueberries
1 cup fresh blackberries

Step Two

3 large egg yolks, at room temperature
3 tablespoons sugar
3 tablespoons Moscato d'Asti, (we prefer Spinetta)

Serves 4

Gently wash berries. Drain and pat dry. Place in dessert glasses.

Place all ingredients in a copper or stainless steel pan with a rounded bottom. Beat with a hand mixer or whisk until foamy. Place pan in a double boiler over medium-high heat and continue beating while moving the pan on and off the heat. (This prevents the mixture from curdling). Hold the corner of the pan with a potholder to keep heat off hands. Continue beating until mixture thickens and doubles in size. Do not over heat. Keep mixture just warm. Pour over berries.

Recommended Wine
Rabbit Ridge Champagne, Moscato d'Asti

Labeling: *We colorized our Paso Robles Westside label in Tuscan shades of gold and butter. We wanted to express the uniqueness of the area by creating a label featuring this special region.*

There are many steps involved in creating a wine label. Coloration, layout, text placement and proportions all have to be determined. Once the label is designed, specific rules apply for getting approval from the government. For example, the appellation must be adjacent or parallel to the varietal; vintage must be near the appellation; alcohol content must be on the front in large type; the name of the wine must be checked for trademark clearance. Because any wine over 14% alcohol costs the winery more in taxes, Rabbit Ridge's oenologist and various lab technicians must spend painstakingly long hours running lab tests to make sure alcohol content is correct for the label.

Mom's Key Lime Pie

My mother makes this key lime pie in the summer when fresh key limes are abundant in Florida. It can also be served as a mousse served in a parfait glass. Instead of using the graham crackers as a crust, sprinkle them on top of the mousse as a garnish.

Step One

18 graham crackers
3 tablespoons sugar
1 tablespoon flour
¼ cup butter, melted

Serves 8

Process graham crackers, sugar and flour. Pour into a bowl and add butter. Stir to combine. Grease a pie pan. Press crust firmly into pan. Bake at 350° for 5 minutes. Cool.

Step Two

3 eggs, separated
1 can sweetened condensed milk
½ cup key lime juice

Reserve egg whites for step three. Whisk egg yolks and lime juice. Add condensed milk and whisk again. Pour into crust.

Step Three

3 egg whites from above, at room temperature
Pinch of sugar

Beat egg whites and sugar until stiff peaks form. Spread on filling. Broil a few seconds until meringue is lightly browned. Chill 1 hour.

Key Lime Mousse: To make key lime mousse, process graham crackers and sugar together. Omit flour and butter. Instead of pouring mixture into crust after step 2, fold whipped egg whites and sugar from step three into lime mixture. Spoon lime mousse into parfait glasses. Sprinkle graham crackers mixture on top and chill for 1 hour. Serve cold.

Poached Peaches with Peach Sorbet

Fresh peaches simmered in sugar, lemon and cointreau are great served over peach sorbet. If I do not have the time to make homemade sorbet, purchase ready-made.

Step One

1 cup water
3 tablespoons sugar
Juice of ½ lemon
Zest of 1 lemon
¼ cup Cointreau

Step Two

3 firm, but ripe peaches, peeled, cored and sliced ½ inch thick

Step Three

4 large scoops of peach sorbet

Serves 4

Simmer water, sugar, lemon juice, lemon zest and Cointreau for 5 minutes. Remove from heat.

Place peaches in sauce from step one and bring to a simmer. Gently stir peaches until tender and the sauce is reduced to syrup. Let cool to room temperature and set aside.

Place sorbet on desserts plates. Cover with peaches and sauce.

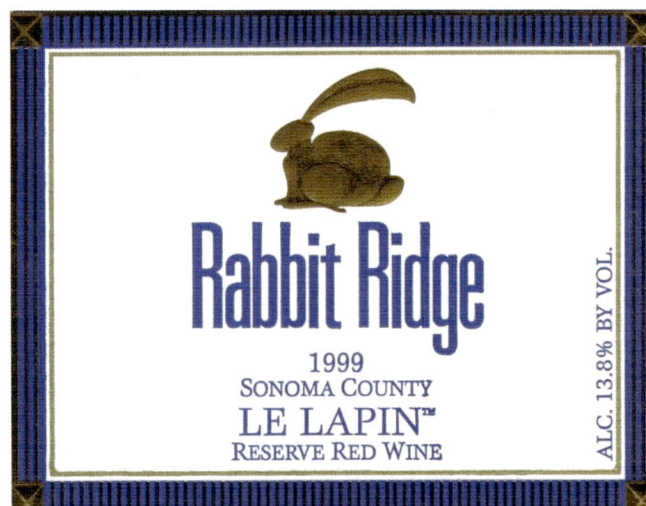

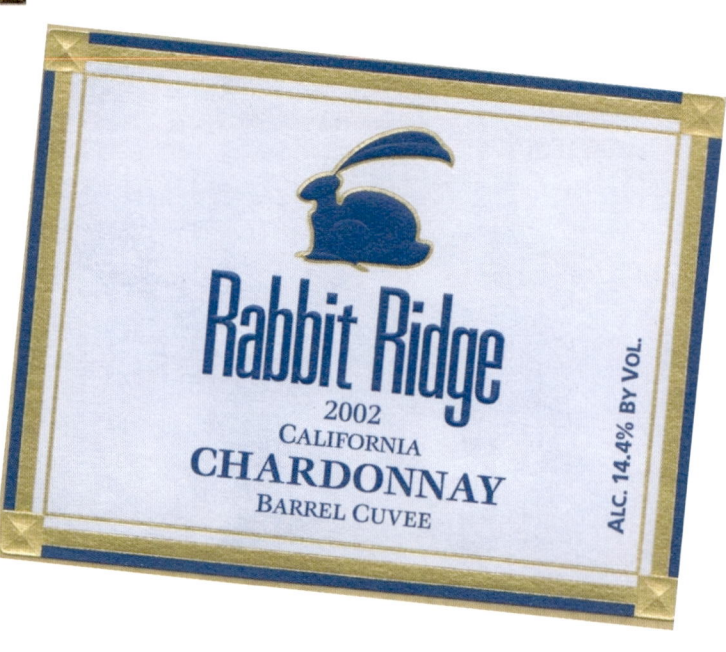

Label Design: *The first proofing stage of a newly designed label is crucial. Once the first cutting is made, future vintages can be changed and reprinted. I am usually present to oversee the procedure because many things can affect color when printing. The degree of pressure made by the label technician can affect the lightness or darkness of the ink. Therefore, a watchful eye is needed. In the case of our 2000 Paso Robles Zinfandel, I wanted the faux yellow to have just enough color to show the light background underneath the darker overlay. Many samples were tested and then reprinted until the exact effect was achieved. It can take hours to get the correct color palette and design. Fortunately, it only took us four hours to get the Paso label right.*

Rabbit Ridge has three different label colorations making up 35 different types of wine.

Pumpkin Custard

I often think of my mother's pumpkin pie she made for the family every Thanksgiving when I smell these pumpkin custards cooking. Although I think fresh is always best, canned pumpkin is a great alternative for this recipe, and it is much quicker than cooking a fresh one. My sister Sandy makes this dessert often.

Step One
½ cup milk

½ cup heavy cream

½ teaspoon vanilla

Step Two
1 egg

2 egg yolks

3/4 cup sugar

Pinch of ground nutmeg

Pinch of salt

½ cup canned pumpkin

Step Three
Whipped Cream for Garnish

Pinch of cinnamon sugar

Serves 2

Heat oven to 350º. Combine milk and cream in a small saucepan and scald. Cool slightly. Add vanilla. Set aside.

In a clean bowl combine 1 egg, yolks, sugar, nutmeg and salt. Beat with an electric mixer for 3 minutes. Add pumpkin and beat 1 more minute. Beat 1/2 cup of egg mixture into milk mixture. Then slowly add entire milk mixture to the egg mixture. Beat a few more seconds. Pour into greased and sugared custard cups or soufflé dishes all the way to the top. Bake 1 hour or until a toothpick come out clean when inserted into the center. Check after 30 minutes. Cool completely. Place in refrigerator until very cold.

Place a dollop of whipped cream in the center of the pumpkin custard; sprinkle a pinch of cinnamon/sugar on top. Serve cold.

Sarah's Strawberry Surprise

When I want something light at the end of a meal, I make this Jell-O dessert. It is low in sugar and fat, yet full of refreshing strawberry flavor. My daughter Sarah loves strawberries. She can eat an entire pint by herself,

---

Step One

1 (3 ounce) package of sugar-free strawberry Jell-O

2 cups water

Step Two

2 egg whites

1 teaspoon Splenda (no calorie sweetener)

Step Three

¼ cup heavy cream, or low fat, sugar- free cool-whip

1 teaspoon splenda, no calorie sweetener

Fresh sliced strawberries for garnish

Serves 8

Prepare Jell-O according to package directions. Stir until Jell-O is completely dissolved. Place in a bowl and refrigerator until slightly thickened.

Whip egg whites with Splenda until stiff peaks form. When Jell-O has thickened slightly, but not set, whisk in egg whites. Make sure to incorporate well.

If using cream, whip with splenda until firm. Fold cream or cool-whip gently into Jell-O mixture until completely combined. Place in decorative parfait glasses. Chill until set, at least 1 hour. If desired, serve with strawberries and more cream on top.

Sarah's Chocolate Chip and Ice Cream Tower

My daughter created this fun dessert. She loves all of these ingredients and wanted to have them all at once. Stacking the ingredients makes it look pretty also. I tried to use low-fat products where I could, for my conscience. However, go full fat, if you like.

Step One Chocolate Sauce

(Ready-made chocolate sauce may be used)

½ **cup fat-free sweetened condensed milk**

¼ **cup unsweetened fat-free cocoa, sifted (wonder cocoa is nice)**

1 **tablespoon real vanilla**

Serves approx. 12

Sift cocoa. Slowly, whisk in condensed milk and vanilla.

Step Two

1 **package of ready bake chocolate- chip cookie dough, sliced**

(You may have extra cookies left over)

Pre-heat oven to 350º. Bake cookies until just done. Let cool 10 minutes. Do not put in the refrigerator or they will get hard. Set aside for step 3.

Step Three

1 **pint of vanilla ice-cream**

½ **pint of fat-free cool-whip**

1 **tablespoon sifted wonder cocoa**

1 **pint of fresh strawberries, hulled cleaned and sliced**

Working quickly, remove ice cream from carton (we cut it off). Wrap ice cream in plastic wrap and place in the freezer for 10 minutes. Remove ice cream and slice ¼ inch thick. Wrap again and place in freezer. When very hard, remove sliced ice cream and cut rounds, the same size as the cookies above (We used a round cookie cutter). Place rounds in the freezer until ready to assemble.

Assembly: When cookies are at room temperature, place one cookie in the center of a dessert plate. Place one ice cream round on top of the cookie. Drizzle with chocolate sauce. Top with a dollop of cool-whip. Sprinkle with sifted cocoa and top with a strawberry slice. Serve immediately.

The Healdsburg tasting room and vineyard is adorned with blooming wisteria.

Rabbit Ridge currently has two tasting rooms and hospitality centers. The first and original is in Healdsburg, California located in Sonoma County. The building is nestled on our rolling hillside vineyard on Westside Road. The second, and home to our new 55,000 square foot winery, is in Paso Robles, in the Central Coast of California. The Paso Robles tasting room is located in the barrel room of the winery for added ambiance. The tasting rooms are a great source of sales and a wonderful way to meet interesting wine lovers and loyal customers.

One of the most important functions of a winery is selling the finished product. Having great distributors is the key to a successful winery. A distributor is the voice and the muscle introducing new and exciting wines to the retailer and the consumer. It takes a lot of work to build a strong relationship with your distributor. Therefore, having a terrific sales manager is crucial. The sales manager's days are long and usually filled with endless details and hundreds of e-mails and telephone calls.

WINE & RECIPE PAIRING INDEX

RECIPE INDEX

REFERENCES

REFERENCE BOOKS

Hugh and Johnson's Pocket Wine Book, Octopus Publishing, London 1977-2001

Cooking Essentials- The Food and Beverage Institute, The Culinary Institute of America

Discovering Wine. Simon & Schuster Inc., Octopus Publishing, Joanne Simon

101 Essential Wine Tips, DK Publishing, Tom Stevenson, 1977

The Vintners Table- Published by Simi Winery, 1998 Mary Evely

Charlie Trotters' Seafood and Meat, Ten Speed Press. Berkeley, CA.

Le Repertoire de la Cuisine, Leon Jaeggi & Sons, London.

The Saucier's Apprentice A Modern Guide to Classic French Sauces, Sokolov, Knopf 1980

Thc Art of Cooking, Jaquqes Pepin, Knopf, 1987

STUDIES

The Culinary Institute of America, Food and Beverage Institute, Techniques of Health Cooking, completed 2002

Introduction to Wine Making- UC Davis, California Class Tapes-

Italian Culinary Institute, Italian Olive Oil Center - Olive Oil Consultants course, completed 2002

International Correspondence Schools, Catering and Gourmet Cooking.